The Gospel for Little Kids

45 Chapel Talks for Children Ages 3-6

THE GOSPEL FOR
Little Kids

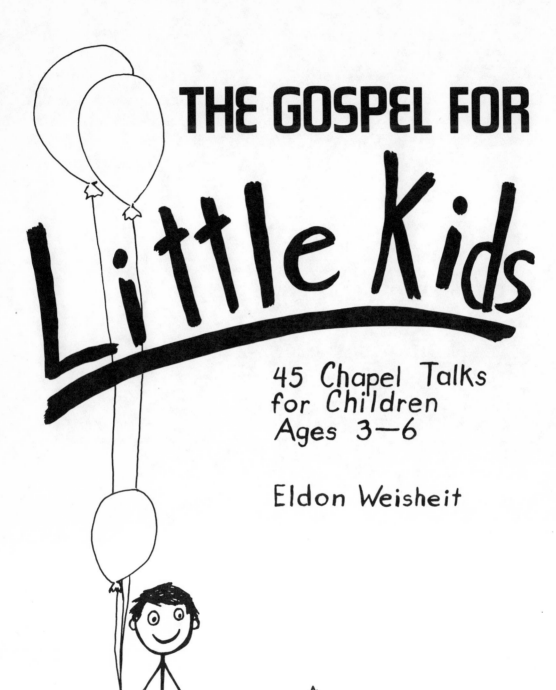

45 Chapel Talks
for Children
Ages 3—6

Eldon Weisheit

Publishing House
St. Louis

Concordia Publishing House, St. Louis, Missouri
Copyright © 1980 Concordia Publishing House
Manufactured in the United States of America

3 4 5 6 7 8 9 10 11 WP 90 89 88 87 86 85 84 83 82

Dedicated to the teachers of the little kids at
Fountain of Life Lutheran School, Tucson, Arizona:
Ruth Heinzelmann, Alice Ludwick, Irene Richmond,
Chris Ries, Joel Schmidt, Mary Schmidt, Roberta Weiss.

Contents

A Word About
The Gospel for Little Kids

In your mind's eye see the story of Jesus blessing the little children. Sunday school pictures often show Jesus out in a park. Mothers have their children out for a stroll. Jesus plays with the kids. A nice afternoon off away from the annoying Pharisees and the crowds of sick people.

Not so.

Jesus blessed the children as a part of His busy and involved ministry to all people. His encounter with the children is in the same section of the script that includes questions such as: Who is the greatest? Does our law allow a man to divorce his wife? What must I do to receive eternal life?

Jesus did not use the children as a diversion from His work. The people brought the children to Him for the same reason they brought others to Him. The children needed Jesus. The disciples objected to His wasting time on the little ones. They couldn't vote. They couldn't contribute. The disciples wanted to get to the decision makers.

"When Jesus noticed this, He was angry and said to His disciples: 'Let the children come to Me, and do not stop them, because the kingdom of God belongs to such as these. I assure you that whoever does not receive the kingdom of God like a child will never enter it.' Then He took the children in His arms, placed His hands on each of them, and blessed them" (Mark 10:14-16).

The devotions in this book are offered as part of a busy ministry of the church today. They are intended for midweek chapel services for preschools and can be adapted for other uses. Devotions directed to the 3- to 6-year-old crowd do not imply that children are more important than others in the church. But children are also a part of the church. They also need the church's ministry.

The devotions are not offered as a way for the children to "play grown-up and go to church just like Mommy and Daddy." Nor are children's worship services a symbol of an affluent society that offers the little ones every luxury.

Ministry to children is an important part of the ministry of a congregation. The rest of the church must let the children come to Jesus and not stop them, because the kingdom of God belongs to them. The rest of the church must receive the ministry of Christ also through children, as adults learn from the kids how to be part of the kingdom of God. The adults who participate in worship services for little children will learn much and, if given the opportunity, contribute much to the Sunday morning worship life of the parish.

9

These devotions are offered as an aid to the teacher or pastor who prepares worship activities for the preschool. As with all worship aids, the messages must be adapted to the needs and abilities of those who worship—both the leader and children. In many cases dialog with the children is written into the message. In all cases dialog will be possible as leader and worshipers develop a partnership in worship.

The devotions are divided into three sections. The first section includes messages for a Christian school year—but not for each week. The second section has messages for special situations in the lives of the students and the classes. These devotions may be scheduled to fill in the weeks not included in the school year devotions. Or they may be used on short notice if the need arises. The third section offers devotions to teach basic spiritual concepts. They are offered as a way of building a foundation for the children's life of worship.

The primary purpose of the devotions is to offer worship experiences for the children. The secondary purpose is to help the children learn to worship by experience. When they become adults, the children will not consciously remember the content of many, if any, of the devotions. But they will remember having been in school chapel. They will remember the feelings they experienced in the worship situation. If they remember rigid, strict rules, or if they remember misbehavior and disregard for God, the worship experiences will have done more harm than good.

Plan each worship service with the awareness that you are contributing to each child's memory bank. Help each of them experience the presence of Christ in worship. Let the attitude that is in Christ Jesus be also in you. Let them see His love in your love. Help them be in a relaxed, accepting atmosphere. Teach them reverence and respect, but teach it in joy and love.

It is difficult to teach the deep theological truths of Christianity to young children. But remember to operate with them on a feeling as well as an intellectual level. They may not understand all the theological details of a message. That will not hurt them as long as they are not quizzed on intellectual content and made to feel guilty because they failed. Small children are used to living in a world where they do not understand the implication of much that is happening. They accept what they are ready for. The Gospel of Christ must always be offered to them. Be careful not to use Law motivations and the power of guilt that will later have to be overcome by correct teaching.

After the Sunday morning worship service, pastors almost always greet the worshipers with words and a handshake. It is a part of the worship service. After a worship service for children, the leader can sit (to be on the same physical level as children) and talk to the children. Some children will want to show something they have. Some will want to talk. Others will want a hug. Some will want to sit on the leader's lap. It is part of a worship service for children.

Do not get the idea that children entering preschool are beginning their education. They have already completed the most important part of the learning process. However, they are entering a new phase of their education.

10

In their first three years they have already learned more than they will during the rest of their lives. Almost all of their learning has been from examples, not programs. Functions such as walking, speaking, and dressing are learned by example rather than program.

Preschool begins the transition of learning from example to learning by programs. Previously the child learned as an individual; now he or she learns in a group. Previously the child learned because he or she saw the need to learn; now the teacher sets the agenda. Previously the child learned mostly by watching; now hearing becomes more important.

The change from learning by example to learning by program is never total. Adults still learn much by example. But part of the maturation process is to gain the ability to learn by program. Education cannot depend on the accident of a good example.

Think of a small child sitting on a parent's lap. They talk about Jesus. The parent tells a Bible story. The child reacts by seeing Jesus in his or her own life. They pray. Now think of a Sunday morning worship service in your church. The same things happen on a corporate basis.

Worship services for preschools are the first step of the transition from the lap to corporate worship. To help children make the change from the one to the other, you must include elements from both experiences. The child must feel the personal attention experienced on the lap. The message of Scripture must be offered on his or her level. It must be interesting enough (that means related to the child's needs) to hold attention. Each child must have the opportunity to feel the touch of Christ.

Each child must also begin to experience corporate worship. Don't just tell children they must be quiet in church. Some adults know only one verse from the Bible about worship, "Be still and know that I am God." Let your children also learn, "Make a joyful noise to the Lord." Let them know when and why good order must exist: "God can hear us pray no matter how much noise someone makes. But if we are going to pray together, we have to listen to one another."

Explain the "whys" of folding hands, standing, kneeling, singing, reading the Bible. Children should not get the idea that going through certain actions is worship. Help them understand that God talks to them and they talk to God. Offer the form as a way of aiding the dialog.

The benefits of worship cannot be measured in the skills of the worship leader. Instead the leader is responsible to bring together the lives of the worshipers and the power of God. The leader must know the Word of God. The leader must know the kids.

Jesus said: "Let the children come to Me, and do not stop them."

THE WORD
Jesus said, "I will be with you always." Matthew 28:20b

I would like for each of you to hold up one finger. Hold your finger in front of your face so you can see it. That finger is part of you. You brought your finger along to school today.

Each of the other boys and girls, and each of the teachers, is also holding up a finger. Keep your finger right where it is, but look at all the other fingers. Because each person is holding up one finger, we can count the fingers and see how many children we have in school. (For a small group, count them. In a larger group tell the group how many are present.)

When you look at all of the fingers, you know you're not alone. But now look just at your own finger. Does it look lonesome? Can you feel alone even when you are with other boys and girls? Sometimes that happens. Sometimes we feel alone at school even though many other kids are here.

Put your finger under your arm. Now no one can see your finger. You know it's there even though you can't see it. Your finger is all by itself. Do you sometimes feel you're all alone?

Bring your finger out so you can see it again. Sometimes we can feel alone even when we're with others. Do you feel alone here at school? When we start a new school year, many boys and girls are afraid. Each of us is doing something new that we have not done before. For some of you, this is your first week in school. All of you are in a new class with a new teacher. Even the teachers are doing something for the first time. They are also new in your class.

When we do something new, we sometimes feel alone—like your finger when you held it under your arm. At school you can't talk to your mother or father. At school you don't have your pet or favorite toy to play with. You're in a new room with new children.

But you're not alone. We come together in chapel so we can all help each other. Hold up your finger again. Look at all the other fingers. Each boy and girl and each teacher is here with you. They are here to help you. And you're here to help them. It's important for you to be here, so the others won't be alone. It is important that the others are here, so you won't be alone.

Someone else is also with you. Jesus is here. He's your Savior. He loves you. Because He loves you, He wants to be with you. He promised us, "I will be with you always."

Look at your finger again. Hold up the second finger with the first. Now your finger is not alone. You can see two. You are one. Jesus is the other. Put your hand under your arm. Your finger is not alone. The one that is Jesus is there too. Wherever the one finger goes, the other goes too.

Jesus is like that. Everywhere you go, He goes with you. He is here in school with you.

Halloween and Reformation

The Word
As they talked and discussed, Jesus Himself drew near and walked along with them; they saw Him, but somehow they did not recognize Him. Luke 24:15-16

The World
A child from the group covered with a sheet. Select and separate this child before the group gathers so the others will not know who it is.

Jesus rose from the dead on a Sunday morning. That night two of His friends went for a long walk. The Bible tells us: "As they talked and discussed, Jesus Himself drew near and walked along with them; they saw Him but somehow did not recognize Him."

Does that remind you of Halloween? On Halloween people put on masks and costumes so others won't know who they are. Jesus didn't wear a mask. But the two friends thought He was dead; so they didn't know Him.

Do you know who this is? (Bring out the child covered with the sheet.) It's someone you all know. You can see how tall the person is. Is this a boy or a girl? You need some clues, don't you? Let's see whose hand it is. (Help the child under the sheet expose a hand.) Does anyone recognize this hand? How about this foot? (Gradually show more and more of the child under the sheet until the others identify him/her.)

I had to help you find out who was under the sheet. I gave you clues. Then you knew it was _____ . Jesus also helped His two friends recognize Him. He gave them clues. First Jesus talked to them about the Bible. He told them why the Savior had to die on the cross to pay for their sins. He reminded them that God had promised that the Savior would come back from the dead.

Each clue that Jesus gave was like seeing a little bit more of the child under the sheet. Finally when Jesus ate dinner with His two friends, they knew who He was. They knew He was the Savior who had died and had come back to life—just as you found out it was _____ under the sheet.

Jesus does not wear a mask to hide Himself from us. He wants us to know Him.

But sometimes we are like those two friends who went for a walk. Sometimes we don't know that Jesus is with us. But He gives us clues so we will know Him. He gives us clues when He forgives us, when He loves us, when He hears our prayers and helps us. When we see the clues, we can know Jesus.

The day we call Halloween is also called Reformation Day. Reformation means that we make something good again. Reformation Day tells us that we can know Jesus. It helps us recognize Jesus as our loving Savior, who forgives us for all the bad things we do. Reformation Day helps us to know that Jesus is with us to help us all the time. Watch for the clues so you can recognize Him.

Thanksgiving

The Word
Give thanks to the Lord, because He is good and His love is eternal. (Psalm 118:1)

The World
The children and things they would have with them in chapel.

The Bible reading for today tells us to give thanks to the Lord. Do you know how to give thanks? Do you know how to give thanks to the Lord? Let's talk about it.

First, let's talk about giving. How do you give something?

Who can give me a shoe?

That's right. Each of you can give me a shoe, because you all have shoes on.

Now who can give me a handkerchief?

Some of you can give me a handkerchief. But some cannot. If you don't have a handkerchief, you can't give me one. You can't give me something you don't have. You can't give thanks unless you are thankful.

I want you to know about Jesus so you can be thankful. If you know that Jesus loves you, if you know He is with you and takes care of you, if you know He forgives all your sins—then you have faith in Him. Then you can give thanks. You can give thanks because you have something to be thankful for.

We've talked about giving shoes and handkerchiefs. It's easy to give them, because you can see them. You can hand the shoe to me and I can take it. But we can't see thanks. So we have to learn how to give something that we cannot see and touch.

I'll show you. Who can give me a hug? I don't see a hug on any of you like I see your shoes. But you can give me a hug, can't you? (Let several children, all if practical, give you a hug.) Hugs are real. You can give them away. But when you give a hug, you don't lose anything. If you gave me your shoe and I took it, you would not have a shoe. But when you give me a hug and I take it, you get a hug too.

We've talked about giving shoes and hugs. Now how do you give thanks? Can you give me thanks now? (Help the children discover they can give thanks by saying "Thank you." Ask them how they give thanks to someone who gives them a present or who helps them.)

The Bible reading says we are to give thanks to the Lord. How do you give thanks to God? (Help the children give examples of how they can say their thanks to God. Example: they can say "Thank you, God," at any time. They say thanks to God at mealtime and evening prayers. They say thanks to God in worship services. They sing thanks to God in hymns.)

We give thanks to God because He is good and He loves us all the time. (Conclude with thanksgiving prayers and songs. Let the children name things for which they are thankful.)

Advent One

The Word

This was the real light—the light that comes into the world . . . John 1:9a

The World

A large candle and matches.

Do you know what this is? (Show candle.)
Do you know what these are? (Show matches.)
What do you expect to happen?
Right—you expect me to light the candle. And I will in a little bit. But first, let's talk about what you're expecting me to do. You're waiting for me to light the candle because candles are meant to be lighted. I can keep a candle for a long time in a box or in a drawer. This candle has been here at church since before we started school last September. That's a long time, isn't it? But it has not been lighted.

But we have waited long enough. Now is the time to light the candle. (Light it.) I like to watch a candle burn, don't you? It's warm and friendly. It makes me think of birthdays and church and Christmas and parties.

A candle can also make us think about Jesus. The Bible says Jesus is a light—a light that comes to the world. Jesus is with us now. Because He was born as a baby and became our Savior, He is a part of our world today. He is with us. He is a light like this candle—a light to show us that God is with us to help us and to love us.

But Jesus was not always a part of the world. (Blow out the candle.) Before Jesus was born the people were waiting for Him to come—like you waited for me to light the candle. They waited and waited for His coming. Each year we also wait to

15

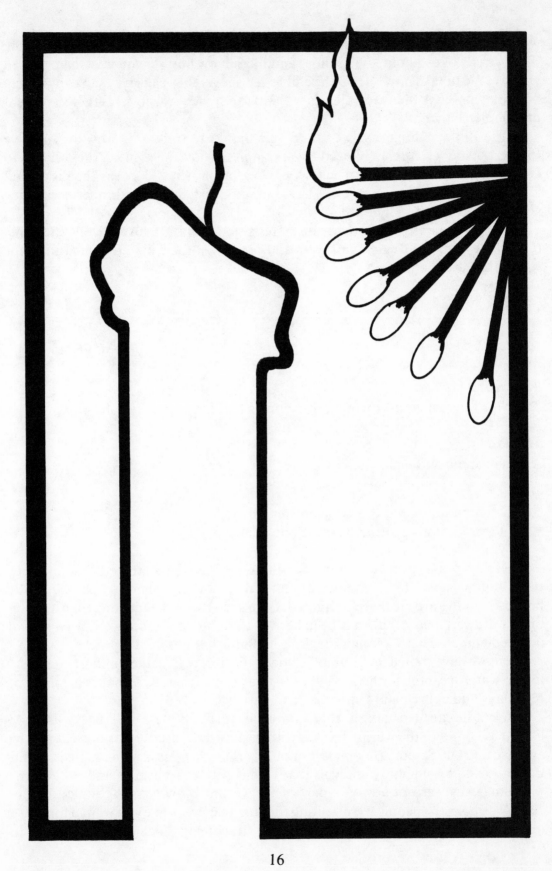

16

celebrate His birthday again. We have only _____ more days until Christmas, the day we celebrate as Jesus' birthday. We're waiting for Christmas to come. We call this time of the year Advent. Advent means "coming." Christmas is coming because Jesus came a long time ago.

A candle that is not lighted can remind you of Advent. The candle with no flame is waiting to be lighted. It's still a candle, but it's not making any light.

Before Jesus was born, God was already God. He loved all people and He wanted to show His love. But He was waiting. He waited until the time came that He sent Jesus to be born as our Savior. Jesus became God's light to show us the way to find Him.

We already have the light, because we know Jesus. (Light the candle again.) But we're waiting for Christmas, when we remember again how He came to us.

Candles will be a big part of Christmas. You'll see real candles and you'll see pictures of candles. Let each candle remind you of God. If the candle is not lighted, remember He is coming and you are waiting for Him. When you see the lighted candle, remember that Jesus is here. He is the Light of the world.

Advent Two

The Word
This was the real light—the light that comes into the world and shines on all mankind. John 1:9

The World
The large candle used last week, matches, other candles of various sizes, shapes, and colors.

What does this candle make you think about? Remember what we said last week? The candle has no flame. It is waiting to be lighted. When you see a candle and matches, you know what to expect. A match will light the candle.

We're also waiting for something else to happen. Remember? Christmas is coming. Long ago, before Jesus was born, the people waited for Him to come to be their Savior. They knew God loved them. They knew He would send Jesus. They were like people who had a candle, but it made no light.

We also are waiting. We're waiting for Christmas. It will come in _____ days. We call this time of the year Advent. Advent means "coming." Christmas is coming.

Then Jesus came. (Light the big candle.) When the candle is lighted, it reminds us of Christmas. Jesus was born. He is the Light of the world. Now the candle makes light. We have a Savior who shows us God.

17

The big candle reminds us of Jesus when it is lighted. But now look at these other candles. See: Some are big, some are little. Some are fat and some are thin. Some are red, some white, some green, some pink. Just as the big candle reminds us of Jesus, the other candles can remind us of ourselves. Like the other candles, some of us are big. Some are little. We have different shapes and different colors. We are different in many ways. But we are all people, just as these are all candles. And as all these other candles have no light, we also by ourselves have no light.

What would you expect to happen if I held the wick of one of the small candles next to the wick of the big candle? That's right. It will be lighted too. And so will this one. And this one. (Light all the other candles.)

During Advent we're waiting for Christmas to come. Because we know God loves us, we expect Jesus to come to us. We know what we're waiting for. The Bible tells us He came to be the Light of the world.

The Bible says that Jesus came to be a light for all of us. When Jesus came to earth, He was like the light that lighted the big candle. When we celebrate Christmas, we come to Him—like the little candles touching the big candle. We know what to expect. We know the little candles will also be lighted. We also know that when we are with Jesus He will give us His light.

As we're waiting for Christmas to come, we're also waiting for something to come to us. Jesus was born a long time ago. But He is still with us today. When we hear the Christmas story, He touches our lives and we receive His light.

He is the Light of the world. He gives us His light.

Christmas

The Word
She [Mary] gave birth to her first son, wrapped Him in cloths and laid Him in a manger. Luke 2:7a

The World
A balloon and a coloring crayon.

Two things in this room are very important. They're so important you could not live without them. But you can't see either of the two things I'm talking about.

You can't see God. He's here. He's with you all the time. But you cannot see God. You need Him. You could not live if there were no God. But you can't see Him.

Another thing in this room that you cannot see is air. You know the air is here. Take a big breath. Feel the air in your chest. Hold your hand in front of your mouth and nose. Let the air out. Feel it. You can feel it, but you cannot see it. If the air were not here, you could not live.

I would like to help you see the air, so you can also know how you can see God. Think of ways that I might help you see the air. I brought a coloring crayon. If I colored the air, you could see it. But look—I cannot color the air. On a cold morning you can see your breath. Then you see the air. But I did not want it to be cold in here.

But I found another way for you to see the air. See—I will put some air in this balloon. (Blow the balloon up.) Now you can see the air in the balloon. The air I breathed out went into the balloon. You can see what the air did to the balloon. You can know it's there. The air has a skin around it. The skin is not the air, but it shows us where the air is.

God also found a way for us to see Him. He became a person like you and me. The Christmas story tells how God made Himself a person, so we could see Him. God's Son—who is true God—was born to a mother named Mary. She and her husband Joseph named the baby Jesus. When Jesus was born, Mary and Joseph could see God. They saw their baby, but God had become human in that baby. God had skin around Him.

Because Jesus was God who became a person, all the people who saw Him also saw God. The shepherds and the Wise Men who came to worship Him knew that the baby was God's Son who came to be their Savior.

Because Jesus came to earth long ago, we can still see God today. We see pictures of God when we see pictures of Jesus. At Christmastime you see mangers with dolls in them to remind you that God came to earth. You also see pictures of Jesus helping people, pictures of Jesus holding children in His lap. You will see pictures of Jesus dying on the cross to pay for our sins. All of those pictures of Jesus show how God came to be with us.

Jesus also becomes a part of you. Because Jesus was born as a person like you, and because He died and rose again, Jesus is a part of your life. When you were baptized, Jesus came into your life. He loves you and stays with you all the time. You cannot see Him with your eyes. But you can see Him with your heart.

The New Year

The Word

Jesus said: "And I will be with you always, to the end of the age." Matthew 28:20b

The World

A stack of mimeo paper, stapler, marker pencil. Write the new year in large numerals on one piece of paper—also the previous five years each on a separate piece of paper. (If this devotion is used for a single class, the teacher might have each student make his own book.)

Happy New Year! This is the name of the new year. (Show it.) Can you read it? What is the new year called? That means Jesus was born about nineteen hundred and _____ years ago. Because we count our years from the time Jesus was born, we call each year "The Year of Our Lord." This is the year of Our Lord 19_____ . we are happy because Jesus will live with us during this year. Let's put a cross on the year (do it) to show that Jesus is with us. The cross reminds us that Jesus is our Savior. Because He died and lives again, He can be with us. He shares this new year with us. He promised us: "I will be with you always, to the end of the age."

But what are you going to do with last year? (Show the page with the previous year.) Do you throw it away? No. Remember it was a year with our Lord too. You have lived several years with Jesus. (Show each of the past years—going back to the year the children were born. If you have several age groups, indicate a different year for each.) Each of the years has been a year with Jesus. (Mark a cross on each of them.)

You don't throw away an old year when you start a new one. All the things you learned and did in that year become a part of your new year. Instead of throwing the old ones away, you keep them together. (Staple the years together, with the new year on top.)

All of the years together tell your life story. You are like a book, and each new year is another page added to your book. This is the page (first from the back) when you were born. On that page you were baptized, ate your first solid food, had your picture taken. On the next page you learned to walk and talk. (Continue through the pages, talking about big events that happened during each year of development.)

Now look at the new year—the new page in the book of your life. What will happen to you this year? Remember the things you learned to do in your other years are still with you. You can walk and talk. You are born. You are baptized. You feed yourself. You dress yourself. Some of you can even tie your shoes. Those things will stay with you all your life. The new things that happen to you this year will be a part of you for all the years you have in the future.

(Add a stack of blank pages to the book.) The book about my life is this thick. Someday yours will be too. All the things that happen to you this year will be a part of your life.

That's why I want you to know it's a year with your Lord. Jesus is with you. He helps you have a good year. He helps you learn to do good things. He forgives the bad things. Jesus will make 19_____ a good year for you. This good year will stay with you all your life.

Valentine's Day

The Word
This is what love is: it is not that we have loved God, but that He loved us and sent His Son to be the means by which our sins are forgiven. 1 John 4:10

The World
A picture of Jesus, a Bible, and a valentine.

Do you know what this is? Sure, it's a valentine. Do you know what the words on the valentine say? You don't have to be able to read to know what a valentine says. All valentines say, "I love you." We send valentines to our friends to show that we love them.

Even though you're not old enough to read, you know the message of valentines. Because you can't read yet, you're not able to know what this book (the Bible) tells you either. This is a Bible. It's God's message to you. If I gave you the book you would not know what God has to say to you, because you cannot read it yet.

But I can read; so let me tell you what God has to say to you. He says: "This is what love is: it is not that we have loved God, but that He loved us and sent His Son to be the means by which our sins are forgiven."

God says we know about real love because we know about His Son Jesus. See this picture. This is Jesus. There are no words on this picture; so you don't have to read it. But the picture has a message from God to you.

God says we know real love when we know Jesus. God did not just send us a message on a valentine that said, "I love you." He did not just send us this book. God sent His Son Jesus to love us. So we don't have to know how to read to know that He loves us. When we see a picture of Jesus, we know that God loves us and came to live with us. He became a person like us. Jesus could go to parties with people. If He were here today, He could eat valentine cookies with us. He could hold us on His lap and hug us.

But Jesus is not here with us in His body today, because He gave us even greater love than that. Because we have done bad things, we need to be punished. But Jesus took our punishment for us. He loved us so much that He even died for us.

But that's not a sad story. It's a happy story because He came back to life again after He had died. He tells us that He loves us so much that even when we die we can come back to life again. When we die we will not come back to live on earth like we do now. But we will live with Jesus in heaven. And we will be with the other people who love Him also.

Because God loves us so much, we can love Him too. But always remember that we love Him because He loves us. He sent His Son to be our Savior. Now we love Him too.

Washington's Birthday

The Word

For rulers are not to be feared by those who do good, but by those who do evil. Would you like to be unafraid of the man in authority? Then do what is good, and he will praise you, because he is God's servant working for your own good. But if you do evil, then be afraid of him, because his power to punish is real. He is God's servant and carries out God's punishment on those who do evil. Romans 13:3-4

The World

Pictures of Washington and the current President. In Canada use present and past national leaders.

Do you know who this is (Washington)? We celebrate Washington's birthday this week. What did he do? (Discuss major facts from his life. Explain that the President is the leader or ruler of our country.)

Do you know who this is (current President)? The President is our ruler. That means he helps make laws that tell us what we must and must not do. God tells us we are to obey the rulers of our country. Do you know other rulers? (Discuss those the children might know: governors, judges, police.)

Why does God give us rulers? Are the rulers our friends? How do we know they are our friends? How do the rulers know we are their friends?

Listen to what the Bible says about the rulers of a country: (read the text). The Bible says you don't have to be afraid of the rulers. The President, the judges, the police are our friends. They are here to help us do good. But it also says that the rulers will punish us if we break the laws of the country. That's why some people are afraid of rulers. They know they have done something wrong. They are afraid they will be punished.

Remember that God also gave us His Son, Jesus Christ, to be our Savior. The rulers of our country can help us only while we live here. They want to help us obey the country's laws. But God sent Jesus to help us live forever. He wants to help us obey God's law. Jesus does not punish us because we disobey God's law. Instead He took the punishment for us. He died in our place. We are forgiven. We will go to heaven.

The rulers of our country cannot die for us They will not take our punishment for us. But they will help us obey the laws. They will help us do good things. When they must punish someone, they do it so our country will be safer for all of us to live here.

When we celebrate Washington's birthday, we thank God that He gave us George Washington and many other rulers in the past. They have helped us have a good country today. But we also thank God for our rulers today. In our prayers we will thank God for our rulers. We will also ask God to help the leaders of our country.

Ash Wednesday

The Word

Jesus said: "The people there would have long ago sat down, put on sackcloth, and sprinkled ashes on themselves, to show that they had turned from their sins!" Luke 10:13b

The World

Two large pictures of the same kite except one has a longer tail, three identical pictures (perhaps church bulletins), a large metal cake pan, and matches.

Look at this picture of a kite. Remember what you see. (Put the first picture down.) Now look at this picture. Is it the same? Is there any difference between this kite and the one in the first picture? (If no one notices the difference, hold up the first picture again. Help them see the difference. Talk about how the kites are alike and how they are different.)

Now look at these two pictures. (Identical pictures.) Are they alike? Are they different? These pictures are exactly the same. I'm going to change just one thing about one of these two pictures. Then I'll see if you can tell the difference. (Hold one of the pictures over the metal pan and burn it.)

Now are the two pictures alike? (Show the picture and the ashes.) How are the

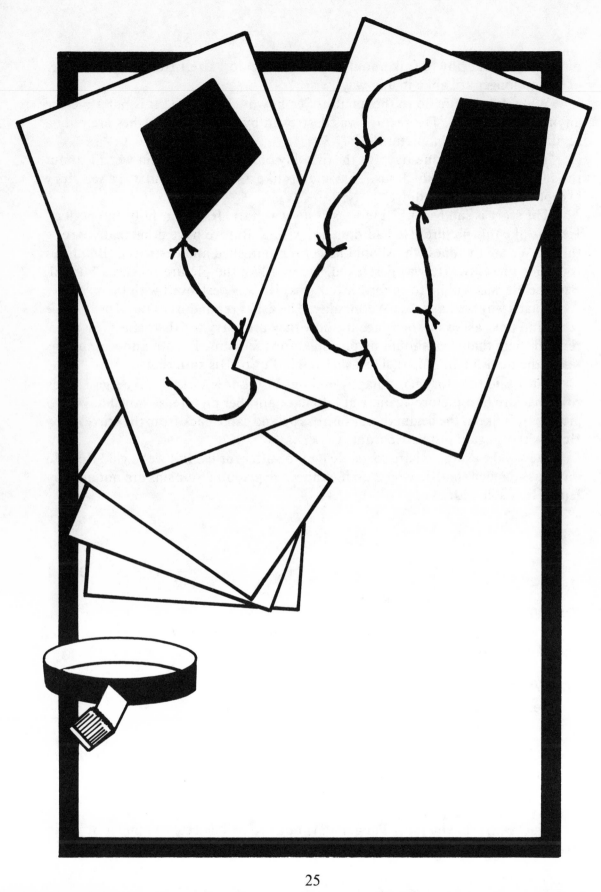

pictures different now? (Talk about difference in color, size.) How are they alike? (They no longer are alike in any way.)

What did the fire do to the picture? See how it changed it? It is not a picture anymore. It is ashes. The picture was destroyed by the fire. The ashes are only a reminder that we had a picture.

Today is Ash Wednesday. It's the first day of Lent. During Lent we talk about the suffering and death of Jesus. That sounds like a sad story. And it is a sad story except it has a happy ending.

The story is sad because it tells us Jesus was hurt. Jesus was holy and perfect. He was like this picture. He had done no wrong. But we have done many wrong things. We are the ones who should have been punished and destroyed. But Jesus took our place. So He was destroyed. He was like the picture that was burned. Because He was willing to suffer for our sins, He was destroyed with them.

That's why we have Ash Wednesday. The ashes remind us of our sins. People sometimes put ashes on their face to show they are sorry for their sins. The ashes remind them that they should be punished for their sins. But we know Jesus has taken the punishment for us. The ashes remind us of His suffering.

But I said the story has a happy ending. You know I can't make these ashes come back to be a picture again. But I do have another picture; so now I have two pictures just like at the beginning. Jesus rose up and came back from the grave. Now He is with us again just as He wants to be.

We see the ashes and are sorry He had to suffer for us. But we're glad that He loved us so much that He would do it. And we're glad that our sins did not destroy Him. He is still with us.

Lent I

The Word
As the time drew near when Jesus would be taken up to heaven, He made up His mind and set out on His way to Jerusalem. Luke 9:51

The World
A large picture of Sallman's *Head of Christ.*

Look at my face and see if you can tell where I'm going. Where do you think I'm going when I look like this? (Smile and beam.) You can tell that I'm happy. I might be going to visit someone I love. I might be going to a party. (Discuss other happy places you might be going.)

Now where do you think I'm going? (Look sad and dejected.) I might be going to a funeral. That would be sad. Or maybe I'm going to visit a sick friend. Or maybe

I'm going to a job I don't like. (Discuss other sad situations. Do not include a trip to a doctor or dentist. If a child mentions either, reply "The doctor [dentist] is our friend. You might look sad when you go to his office, but you would look happy when you leave because he helps you.")

Now look at this picture. Do you know who this is? That's right. This is Jesus, our Savior. Can you tell me some things about Jesus? (Talk with the children about some details from His life. Include His birth, baptism, some of His miracles.)

Can you tell where Jesus is going when you look at this picture? Is He going to a happy place? Or to a sad place? Does He want to make this trip? How do you think He feels?

An artist painted this picture after he had read this Bible verse: "As the time drew near when Jesus would be taken up to heaven, He made up His mind and set out on His way to Jerusalem."

Jesus knew that if He went to Jerusalem the people would kill Him. He knew that He was walking toward the cross. Can you see the sadness in His face? He was thinking about the pain of the cross. He was thinking about the friends who would run away from Him. He was thinking about the people who would laugh at Him. Jesus knew where He was going when He made up His mind to go to Jerusalem. It was a sad trip.

But look at the picture again. Can you see some happiness too? Jesus is not smiling. But He is glad that He can go to the cross to pay for our sins. He did not die on the cross because the soldiers caught Him and He couldn't get away. He gave His life. The Bible verse says He knew it was time for Him to be taken up to heaven.

When He saw the cross, Jesus was sad. But He looked beyond the cross and saw heaven. He knew that someday we would be in heaven with Him, so He was willing to go to the cross. So the sad trip was also a happy trip.

During Lent we think about the way Jesus suffered and died. But we also look beyond the cross to see heaven. We see how Jesus won the victory over death for us. He is happy that He can love us. We are happy that we can love Him.

The Word

Jesus said: "Now My heart is troubled—and what shall I say? Shall I say, 'Father, do not let this hour come upon Me'? But that is why I came—so that I might go through this hour of suffering." John 12:27

The World

The children as they participate in the devotion.

How did you get ready for school this morning? (Talk about getting out of bed, washing, brushing teeth and hair, and dressing.) If we did not have school today, you might have stayed in bed longer. Or you might not have put on the clothes you're wearing today. (Comment on something special that a student or teacher might be wearing for school and point out it was part of getting ready for school.)

Did you bring something to school with you? (Lunch, show and tell items, note from parents, etc.) Remembering to bring that was part of getting ready for school. Now that you are ready and are here, we have school.

Would it be strange if you got ready for school and came, and then we had no school? Here you are: out of bed, clean and dressed with everything you need for a day at school—but no school. Don't worry—we are having classes today. You are ready. The teachers are ready. So we will have school.

Jesus, too, got ready to do something. He may have gotten ready for school when He was a child. But later He also got ready to die on the cross to pay for our sins. Lent is a special time of the year when we see how Jesus got ready to die for us. When we see how He got ready to be our Savior, we can also get ready to worship Him as the One who died and lives again.

Jesus got ready to be our Savior by becoming a human being—a person like us. He was tempted to sin, He got hungry and thirsty, He cried when He was sad. He had a mother. He had friends. He was a person like us.

Jesus also got ready to die for us by showing that He was also God. He healed sick people. He made dead people become alive again. The people who saw what He did knew He was God.

When He was ready to die for us, He said: "Shall I say, 'Father, do not let this hour come upon Me'?" At the last minute He wondered if He should ask God to keep Him from dying. He thought about running away from the cross.

But Jesus knew He was ready to die for us. So He did not run away. He said: "But that is why I came—so that I might go through this hour of suffering." He knew

28

He would be hurt. He knew He would die. But he was ready. We needed a Savior to pay for our sins. He was here to do it. So He died for us.

Just as you get ready for school and then come to school, Jesus got ready to die for our sins and then did it. We're getting ready to have Good Friday and Easter. As we get ready, we're glad to remember that Jesus got ready too.

Holy Week

The Word

Then [Jesus] bowed His head and died. John 19:30b

The World

Six large pieces of paper on which are printed: 1, 2, A, B, Death, Life.

I want to play a game with you. It is called: "Which comes first?"

Look at this piece of paper (1). What does it say? Now look at this (2). What does it say? Which comes first? Do the two pieces of paper go together this way (hold them to show 2 . . . 1)? Or do they go together this way (1 . . . 2)? One comes first. Then two. See, you are learning to play the game "Which comes first?"

Now look at this paper (A). What does it say? Then look at this one (B). What does it say? Which comes first? Do the two pieces of paper go together this way (B . . . A) or this way (A . . . B)? A comes before B; so A is first.

Let's play the game one more time. See this word (DEATH)? You have not learned to read this word yet, so I will help you. It is death, D . . . E . . . A . . . T . . . H. Do you know what death means? Death is the opposite of life. Anyone who is not alive is dead. One who is dead does not move or talk. He cannot laugh or grow.

We call this Holy Week. During this week a long time ago, Jesus died. He was dead. He died on a cross to pay for our sins. Because Jesus died for us, we don't have to be afraid of death.

When we know Jesus died for us, we can talk about death. You may have had a pet that died. Some of you have had a grandmother or grandfather who died. You can understand death. You know about it.

Remember we're still playing the game called "Which comes first?" You know the word "Death." Now I will teach you another word—this one (LIFE). Do you know what this word is? It is the opposite of death. That's right—it is life, L . . . I . . . F . . . E. Life means to be alive, to be living. You have life. I have life. We can talk and laugh. We can walk and jump. We can learn and grow.

Now which comes first? Is it death first, then life? Or life first, then death? The pet you had was alive first, then dead. That makes it seem that life comes first, then death. We are alive now, but we will die. So death must be last.

But remember the story of Holy Week. Jesus died on Friday. But on the next Sunday He was alive again, and has been alive ever since. In Jesus life comes again after death, and He has promised us that we also will live again.

If we were alone we would have life first, then death. But in Jesus we have life now. Even when we die, we will still have life, because we will live again in Him.

Easter

The Word

But the truth is that Christ has been raised from death, as the guarantee that those who sleep in death will also be raised. 1 Corinthians 15:20

The World

A box of tissues.

See this tissue sticking out of the box? Watch it carefully. I'm going to take it out of the box and throw it away. (Do it.) I threw that tissue away. But look. Here's another one.

I'll throw this one away too. Look. Here's another. And another. And another. Each time I pull a tissue out of the box, another tissue appears. Of course, you know this is not magic. The box says it has 200 tissues. That means for 200 times I can pull out one tissue and another appears. That's good, 'cause when you have a cold and need tissues, you always need lots of them.

But now look at these tissues and think about the Easter message. The Easter message is that Jesus rose from the dead. He had died and had been put in a grave. He was like a tissue in a box. But He came out of the grave. He popped right up and was alive again.

That's an exciting story. Someone was dead and is alive again. But that's not all of the story. It becomes even more exciting than that. Our Bible reading says: "But the truth is that Christ has been raised from death, as the guarantee that those who sleep in death will also be raised."

When Jesus came back from the dead, He opened the door of every grave. Because He died and returned to life, we also can come back to life after we die. We are like the other tissues in the box. Jesus is the first one. Look what happens when I pull out the first one very slowly. See—it makes the way for the second one to come out of the box too. His resurrection from the dead is the guarantee that we also will be raised from the dead. Because His death paid for the sin that causes our death, we don't have to stay dead anymore.

We will still have to die. We will be buried. Jesus also died and was buried. But we won't have to stay dead. Because He arose from the dead, so will we.

31

I imagine that you use tissues many times. Each time you use a tissue, check what happens when you pull it from the box. As you take out one, it pulls the second one up ready to be used. Then remember Easter. Jesus came out of the grave. When He died, He made you like the second tissue. You too will be able to come out of the grave.

Mother's Day

The Word
Children, it is your Christian duty to obey your parents, for this is the right thing to do. Ephesians 6:1

The World
Candy box, flowers, Mother's Day card.

Next Sunday is Mother's Day. Next month is Father's Day. Since we will be on vacation and not in school when Father's Day comes, let's talk about both Mother's and Father's Day today.

First, all of us have a father and mother. Not all of us live with both our father and mother, but each person has, or has had, a father and a mother. If you live with only a father or mother, you can think about that one parent now. Or if you have someone who takes the place of your father or mother, you may think about that person as we talk about Mother's and Father's Day.

What will you do for your parents on that special day? Sometimes children give candy or flowers, like these, to parents on those special days. Some children will buy or make a special card, like this, or a present for their parents.

Mothers and fathers like to receive gifts from their children. They especially like the gifts their children make for them. (Talk about class projects that include gifts for parents.)

Our Bible reading for today tells about something else that you can give to your parents on Mother's and Father's Day—and on all other days. Let me read it to you: (Read the text.)

The Bible says you are to obey your parents. Do you know what "obey" means? (Give the children an opportunity to define "obey." Use some examples: "Fold your hands." "Sit up straight.")

God says it is your duty to obey your parents. That means it's part of your job to do what your parents tell you to do. Your father and mother have duties. They work at jobs. They buy and fix meals for you. They give you clothes and a place to sleep. They bring you to church and school. Those are their duties.

32

Your duty is to obey your parents. It's part of your job. You have a special reason to obey your parents. The Bible says it's your *Christian* duty to obey your parents because it's the right thing to do.

You are a Christian. God gave you His Son to be your Savior. When you were baptized, God made you a Christian. You were washed clean in the name of Christ and you are known by His name, so you're a Christian.

Because you're a Christian you have love to give to your parents. You can obey them not because you will be punished if you don't but because you love your parents.

You may give your father and mother a special gift or card on their special days. But every day you can give them something even more important. You can give them your love by obeying them.

Ascension

The Word

[Jesus] was taken up to heaven as [the disciples] watched Him, and a cloud hid Him from their sight. They still had their eyes fixed on the sky as He went away, when two men dressed in white suddenly stood beside them and said, "Galileans, why are you standing there looking up at the sky? This Jesus, who was taken from you into heaven, will come back in the same way that you saw Him go to heaven." Acts 1:9-11
They . . . went back into Jerusalem, filled with great joy. Luke 24:52
"I have been given all authority in heaven and on earth. . . . I will be with you always. . . ." Matthew 28:18, 20

The World

A golden crown (cut from yellow construction paper or from cardboard colored yellow) and a chair.

Let me read you the story from the Bible that tells us how Jesus left the earth and went to heaven. Remember that He had died for our sins. Then He came back to life. Forty days later He went up to heaven. This is the story: (Read Acts 1:9-11 as given in THE WORD).

You would think that, after Jesus left, His friends would be sad, lonely, and afraid. But the Bible tells us that "They . . . went back into Jerusalem, filled with great joy."

How is that possible?

I have something here that can help us understand the way the disciples felt. (Show crown). What is this? Yes, it's a crown. Who wears a crown? Kings and queens do.

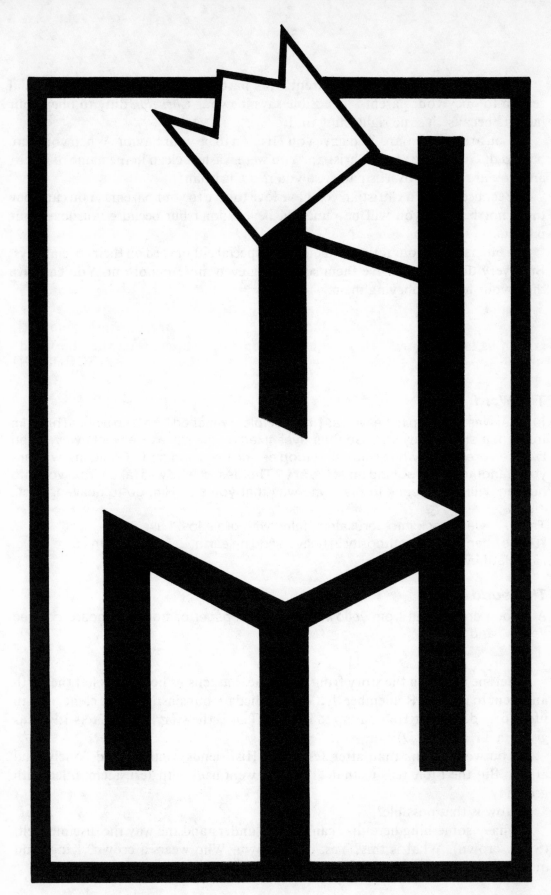

What has a crown got to do with Jesus going to heaven? Well, His ascension—that's a big word for His going to heaven—was really like the crowning of a king.

Let's have a crowning right here. Billy, would you like to come up here? OK. That's fine. Let me place this crown on your head. Now everybody can see that Billy is a king. And now, Billy, sit down here on your throne. (Billy sits down on a chair.)

I think you're starting to see why the disciples were happy instead of sad when Jesus went up to heaven. They knew that in heaven Jesus would be crowned king and would sit on His glorious throne. They also knew that as their king He would help them in every way.

But if Jesus went up to heaven, does that mean that He is far away from us? No. He is close by. Not long before His ascension He said: "I will be with you always." Remember, Jesus is true God. That means He can be wherever He wants to be. He is here with us right now, although since His ascension we can't see Him anymore. He is with us in our homes. He is with His people in a special way when the Lord's Supper is celebrated in church. You'll learn more about that when you get a little older.

Now we can't see Jesus, but in the story I read to you from the Bible the angels said: "Jesus . . . will come back in the same way that you saw Him go into heaven."

Alright, Billy, go back to your seat. Keep your crown on your head. That reminds us that Jesus, our King, will someday come back to us. What a great day that will be!

Last Week of School

The Word
May the grace of the Lord Jesus Christ be with you all. Philippians 4:23.

The World
An empty box.

School is almost over for this year. (Mention the big events, picnic, program, etc., that have or will happen to mark the end of the year.) Soon you will have finished this important year of school.

What will you take with you when you leave school? I have this box. See—it's empty. I'd like each of you to pretend it's your box. You can put things in it that you will take with you from this year of school.

First you may put in some pictures that you drew or colored while you were in school this year. You may put in some books, some of your homework. (Let the students add other material things that they will take home with them.)

You can pretend you're putting books and papers in this box. But you'll take other things with you that can't be put in this box. For example, you learned many things in school this year. Some of you learned how to count. You learned letters from the alphabet. You learned songs and Bible stories. You learned new games. You'll take those things with you. You can't put them in this box, but they're in your mind and they'll go with you.

You can also take good memories with you. You've made friends here. We've had fun together. (Recall special big school events.) You can carry those good memories with you for the rest of your life.

I'd like to read something to you from the Bible that tells you about something else you can take with you. These words are at the end of a book of the Bible, just as we are at the end of our school year. St. Paul, who wrote this book, wanted to remind the people of one last thing. He wanted to give them one more thing to take with them. He wrote: "May the grace of the Lord Jesus Christ be with you all."

I want you to take many things with you from this year of school. I want you to take the things you've learned. Take the good memories. But most of all take the grace of the Lord Jesus Christ.

Remember, grace is God's gift of love to you. God gave you His Son, Jesus Christ. Christ gave His life for you. He gave Himself so you could be with Him forever.

When you take God's grace with you, you are taking the greatest gift God has for any of us. This gift will help you in school next year. It will help you as you grow to be a teen-ager and an adult. By the grace of Jesus Christ you will go to heaven.

May the grace of the Lord Jesus Christ be with you all.

The Word for Special Situations

School devotions are to be planned to fill the needs of the students—not the staff. The devotions should be about topics the children are aware of. Just as Jesus is a part of their family life and school activities, so also the events from the family and school are to be a part of their worship experiences.

When a special situation affects the entire school, it should be included in the chapel services. Prayers of thanksgiving and requests may be included in any chapel service. Current events may be included in many devotions as examples or applications. Or a special devotion may be prepared on a subject that is already on the minds of the children.

A special event that affects one student may also influence the others. Sickness, death, birth, and the like in the family of one child make the other children think about the possibility of such events in their own families. A devotion on the subject helps the children share their joys and sorrows with one another.

The devotions in this section are about special situations that can happen in the life of a family, school, or congregation. Some of these devotions may be scheduled ahead of time to fill anticipated needs. Others may be used on the spur of the moment when the need arises. Do not let a good, pre-planned chapel schedule prevent you from making last-minute changes to bring the comfort of the Gospel to a current need.

These devotions may also be used as examples for you to prepare your own devotions for special situations in your school.

A New Kid in School

The Word
[Jesus said:] "I was a stranger and you received Me...." Matthew 25:35b

The World
This devotion is to involve all the children, not just the new student(s). If your school receives many new students during the year, use this devotion after several have arrived. Review it later as others enroll.

We have some special kids with us today. Do you know who the special people are? You are the special person I'm talking about. Some of you are special because you've been in school ever since we started last September. I'm glad you're in school. I like to see you in class. I like to see you when you come to worship Jesus with all of us.

Some of you are special because you are new in our school. (Name the new student[s] and introduce by name and class.) All of us want to welcome the new student(s) today. I'm glad you're in our school. I want to get to know you. All of us like to have you with us when we come to listen to God's Word, to pray to Him, and to sing our songs of praise.

Jesus tells us we are to welcome strangers. To those of us who have been here since school started, the new student(s) is a stranger. We do not know you. To the new student(s) the rest of us are strangers. You do not know us.

But we won't be strangers to each other very long. We'll all be friends. We're like each other in many ways. God has created all of us; so we're all made the same way. We all know we have done wrong things. But Jesus loves us anyway and He forgives us. So we are all forgiven.

We are alike in some ways. And we are different from one another in other ways. (Talk about the similarities and the differences in the group. Consider: race, male, female, color of hair and eyes. Ask if some are left-handed. Some tall, some short. Show that the new student[s] is like some of the others, and that some of those who have been in school are different from others.)

We're not strangers when we know each other. When we know one another, we know how we are alike and how we are different. When we do things together, we get to know one another. You study together in your classroom and you learn the same things. You play together and get to know one another. You also eat together. Jesus shares with you when you study, play, and eat. He knows each of you and helps you know one another.

We also pray together. Jesus tells us He is with us when we gather together in His name. Let's pray to Him now, to show that we are all friends together and that Jesus is also our friend. (In the prayer include both the new student[s] and the others. Pray also for the Holy Spirit to remove any other barriers that exist between the students.)

We can also sing together. When we sing our songs in chapel, we are talking to God. We share our feelings together. (Sing a song regularly used in chapel.)

We're glad all of you are here in school. We want you to learn how to welcome strangers in Jesus' name as He also has welcomed you.

You Are in a Family

The Word
Children, it is your Christian duty to obey your parents, for this is the right thing to do. "Respect your father and mother" is the first commandment that has a promise added: "so that all may go well with you, and you may live a long time in the land." Parents, do not treat your children in such a way as to make them angry. Instead, raise them with Christian discipline and instruction. Ephesians 6:1-4

The World
Large box of balls—from as many games as possible.

What is that? That's right. It's a ball. What is this? That's a ball too. Is it like the other ball? How is it the same as the first ball? How is it different?

(Continue to show a variety of balls. Compare the largest and the smallest. Show a football and note it is not round. Show a heavy bowling ball and a light ping-pong ball. Look at the different colors. Some bounce and some don't.) But all are balls.

Now let's think about a family. What is a family? A family has a father. Okay, Jeff, you stand here and pretend you're the father. Who'll be the mother? Okay, Jill is the mother. A family has children. Karen, you be a sister; and Jim, you be a brother. Now that is a family. The Bible tells us that children are to learn from their

parents and parents are to teach their children. That could happen in this family.

But this is only one kind of family. We said that all balls are not alike. Are all families alike? How could the family be different?

Some families could have more children. Let's see who comes from the family with the most children. (Talk about the different numbers of children in a family.) Do some of you come from a family with no other children? Do you know a family with no children at all? (Remind them of grandparents.)

If a family has one child or many children, the parents can teach the family about Jesus. If you are the only child, or if you have many brothers and sisters, you can still learn in your family that Jesus loves you and lives with you. If a couple has no children, they can still love one another and share their love with other people. They can love and help other children. They can still be a family.

Some families have only one parent. Either the father or mother may have died, or the parents may be divorced. But they are still a family. The one parent still teaches the love of Jesus. The children still learn from the mother or the father.

Can you think of other kinds of families? (Talk about grandparents, cousins, etc., who might live with a family. If one of your students has a special situation, a foster child for example, include that example of a family.)

Remember all the different kinds of balls. We need different kinds of balls to play different kinds of games. Each of us also need our family. And each of our families need us. When Jesus was on earth, He was part of a family. You are part of a family. Because Jesus is your Savior, He can be part of your family too.

When They Get Angry

The Word

Get rid of all bitterness, passion, and anger. No more shouting or insults. No more hateful feelings of any sort. Instead, be kind and tender-hearted to one another, and forgive one another, as God has forgiven you through Christ. Ephesians 4:31-32

The World

A platter with two pieces of bread, peanut butter, cheese, a piece of carbon paper, and shoestrings.

Do you like sandwiches? I do. Especially when I can make a sandwich for myself. I've got some things to make a sandwich here. I'll let you tell me how to make a nice snack.

First two pieces of bread. Now what shall I put between them? How about this (carbon paper)? (Make a sandwich with it.) Would you eat this sandwich? It would taste bad and make your mouth dirty.

How about a shoestring sandwich? (Put strings between bread.) No—you couldn't chew shoestrings, could you?

Let's throw away the carbon paper and shoestrings. Instead we'll make a sandwich with this. Let's see, some peanut butter and cheese. Now this is a good sandwich.

Let's make a people sandwich. A people sandwich is called friendship. (Ask two children to help.) Mike and Renee are like two pieces of bread. Let's see what we can put between them to make a friendship.

Suppose we put anger between them. What if Mike called Renee bad names? What if she laughed at him? What if he broke her toys? Or she called him dumb? Would they be friends? No. Remember the bread with carbon paper or shoestrings between the slices. That was not a sandwich. Friends cannot hurt one another. We threw away the carbon paper and shoestrings. Our Bible reading says: "Get rid of . . . anger. No more shouting or insults. No more hateful feelings of any sort."

If Mike and Renee have anger or hatred between them, they do not have a friendship. Let's try again.

Let's put kindness and love between Mike and Renee. They say good things to one another. They help one another. Now they have a friendship. Two pieces of bread with peanut butter between them make a sandwich. Two people with love and kindness between them make a friendship. The Bible says: "Be kind and tender-hearted to one another, and forgive one another, as God has forgiven you through Christ."

What do you put between yourself and other people? Do you say mean things to others? Do you hurt others? That will not make a sandwich.

Instead remember what Jesus has given you. He loves you. He forgives you. He is kind to you. Use those gifts from Jesus to make friends with other people. When you're kind to another person, that person will be your friend. When you help people and say good things to them, they'll be your friends.

Remember how to make a good sandwich. Then think about people sandwiches. Put Jesus between you and others. Then they'll be your friends.

When They Use Bad Language

The Word
We use it [the tongue] to give thanks to our Lord and Father and also to curse our fellow-man, who is created in the likeness of God. Words of thanksgiving and cursing pour out of the same mouth. My brothers, this should not happen! James 3:9-10

The World
A bowl of pudding, a bowl of mud, a bowl of clean soapy water, a spoon.

Do you like pudding? I have a dish of pudding. I don't have enough to give each of you a bite. I only have one spoon. Pretend I'm giving you a bite. (Take a spoonful and eat it.)

Now would you like a bite of this (mud)? This is mud, wet dirt. (Hold up a spoonful.) I don't want to eat the mud. Do you? The pudding is good for you. But this is not good for you.

So I'll take another bite of pudding instead. (Dump out the mud and with the dirty spoon take a spoonful of pudding from one side of the bowl and hold the spoon up.) Do you want this bite? I don't. (Let the children talk about why they would not eat from the dirty spoon.)

Now listen to what our Bible says. (Read the text.) The Bible says we use our tongue to say good things—that's like eating the pudding. But we use the same tongue to say bad things. That's like using the same spoon to eat pudding and mud.

We could get two spoons. We could use one for pudding and one for mud. But I only have one tongue. How many tongues do you have? (Check tongues.)

We have to use the same tongue for everything we say. We can use our tongue to say good things. We can use it to thank God and to tell others about Jesus.

But what happens when we say bad words with our tongue? The Bible says we should not use our tongue to say both good and bad things.

Look at the spoon again. It is dirty. But it can be clean again. (Wash it.) Now I can eat the pudding with the spoon. (Do it, from the clean side of the bowl.)

Now think about the tongue. Jesus died to forgive our sins. He makes us clean. We try not to say bad things. When we do say bad things, we ask Jesus to forgive us. When He forgives us, it is the same as when I washed the spoon. We can again use our tongue to say good things about God and about people.

When you say bad things, remember Jesus. He still loves you. He will make you clean. Then you can say good things. And He will help you not to say the bad things again.

When Trouble Comes

(Use this devotion after a tragedy in the congregation or community or after a national calamity that has received wide TV coverage.)

The Word

[God says:] "Call to Me when trouble comes; I will save you, and you will praise Me." Psalm 50:15

The World

Telephone and phone book.

Do you know how to use a telephone? Tell me some of the ways you've used the phone. (Mention conversations with family and friends, information about school, etc.)

We often use the phone when we're in trouble. Have you or your parents used the phone when you were in trouble? (Discuss phoning for repairs, calling a doctor, fire department, police, etc. Mention special tragedy in the area.)

When you're in trouble and you have to call someone, you use this book to look up the number. The doctor's phone number is in the phone book. Think of other numbers in the book that you might look up when you have a problem. (Mention the church phone.)

When you use the phone to call for help, you have to look up the number in the phone book. This book (the Bible) also tells you whom to call when you're in trouble. (Read the text. Say it phrase by phrase; have the children repeat it. Help the children say the verse together.)

How do you call God? Do you need a phone? (Talk about prayer.) Do you need to know the right number?

Of course not. You call God each time you pray. You do not need a special number. But you do need to know God. You need to know that God loves you and listens to you. You know God's number when you know He sent Jesus to be your Savior. Jesus is God's Son living with us. Because you know Jesus, you can talk to God any time.

You can ask Jesus to help any time you have a problem. Do you have a problem now? We will pray about it. (Let the children share their needs. Help them also think of the problems of others—including the community tragedy.)

God has invited us to call on Him when trouble comes. Let's pray now and ask Him to help us and others. (Pray about the items mentioned by the children.)

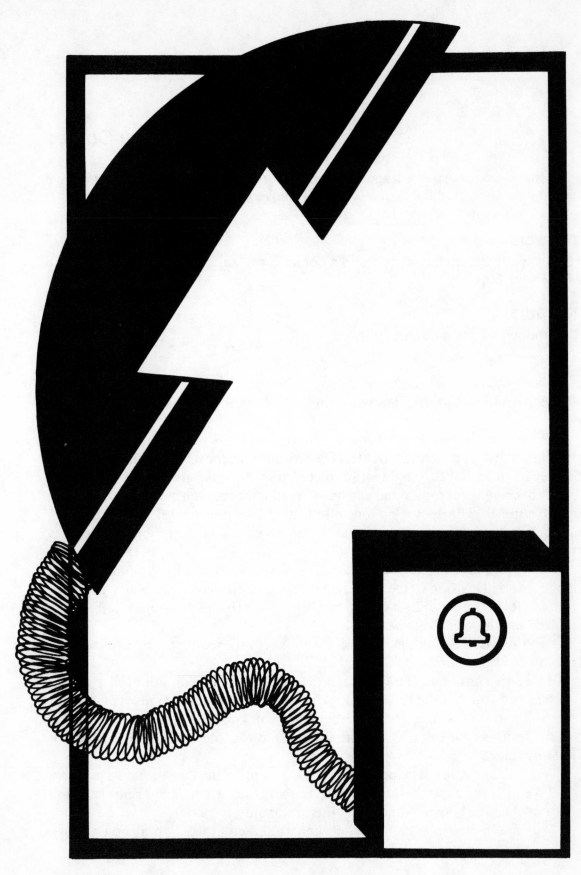

44

Remember, God also said that after He helps us we can praise Him. Can you think of ways that God has answered our prayers? (Mention answers to previous prayers, for food, forgiveness, etc.) We called on God to ask Him to help us. Now let's call on God to thank Him for the help He has already given us. (Close with a prayer of praise.)

When Good Things Happen

(Use this devotion to celebrate a special blessing—maybe the first beautiful day of spring, or when someone gets married, or when something good happens to a family, the congregation, or community.)

The Word
Be joyful always, pray at all times, be thankful in all circumstances. This is what God wants from you in your life in union with Christ Jesus. 1 Thessalonians 5:16-18

The World
A piece of child's clothing, food, toy.

See this sweater? I want it to make you think of all the clothing you have at home. Think about shirts and dresses, hats and coats, socks and shoes. Who gave you your clothing? (Let the children answer. If they say God, agree and ask if God gave the clothing through a person. What person?)

Now look at this apple. I want it to make you think of the food you eat. Think about breakfast, lunch, dinner, snacks. Who gives you your food? (Again lead the children to see that their food comes from parents or whoever is taking care of them.)

Now look at this toy. Think of all the fun things you have. Think about books, TV, and games. Who gives you the fun things of life? (Help the children think of parents and others who have given them gifts.)

Do you know why your parents (and/or others) give you clothing, food, and toys? They give them to you because they love you. They know you need some of the things. They know you enjoy all the things. Your parents want you to enjoy the things they give you.

God also gives you good things. The clothing, food, and toys may come from your parents, but God helps them so they can give them to you. And God gives you your parents and others who love you. (Mention special good events.) God even gave you Jesus to be your Friend and Savior.

Do you know why God gives you all these good things? Because He loves you. He wants you to enjoy life. He wants you to be happy. Listen to what the Bible says: (Read the text.)

God wants you to be joyful. He wants you to pray to Him. You know you can pray to God to ask Him for help when you have a problem. But you can also pray to God when you are happy. You can thank Him. You can tell Him that you enjoy all the good things in the world.

Remember, the Bible says God wants you to be happy in your union with Jesus. "In union with" means you and Jesus are together. He is with you and shares in your life. When you have a problem, He helps you—because He wants you to be happy. Sometimes Jesus takes the problem away. Sometimes He helps you see that He has given you many happy things in life. He does not want the problems you have to take away your joy about the good things. That's why He stays with you.

When Someone Is Sick

(Use this devotion when someone from the school is seriously ill or has been injured in an accident.)

The Word

[Jesus'] disciples asked Him, "Teacher, whose sin caused him to be born blind? Was it his own or his parents' sin?" Jesus answered, "His blindness has nothing to do with his sins or his parents' sins. He is blind so that God's power might be seen at work in him." John 9:2-3

The World

A get-well card for the sick person—perhaps made by some of the students.

One time Jesus and His friends met a person who was blind. Shut your eyes and pretend you are blind. What color is my shirt? Could you find the drinking fountain? If you were blind, you could not do many things that you enjoy. Now open your eyes.

You were not really blind. But that man was. Jesus' friends wondered why he was blind. They asked, "Whose sin caused him to be born blind? Was it his own or his parents' sin?" They thought God must have punished the man by making him blind.

But Jesus said no. He said God did not punish the man or his parents by making him blind. Instead Jesus said the man's blindness would help show God's power at work with people.

Someone from our school is sick today. (Briefly talk about the sickness. Give an honest evaluation of the person's condition and possible results.)

Do you think God made _____ sick to punish him (her) for sin? Of course not. Remember the man who was born blind. God did not punish that man. Instead Jesus healed him. After Jesus talked to him, the blind man could see again. He could

see like you can see. Jesus loved the man and wanted to help him; so He healed him.

_____ is not ill because God is punishing him. Jesus loves _____ . This sickness can also show God's power with us today. In our prayers today we will pray for _____ . We will also pray for others who are sick.

God can and does heal people today. God has given us doctors and medicine. We have a good hospital. We thank God for the help He gives us and our friends when we are sick.

We can also show our love for _____ when he is sick. See this card. We'll send it to _____ in the hospital. The card shows him that we love him too. It will remind him that we also are praying for him.

Jesus shows us that He forgives our sins. He does not punish us by making us sick. When someone does get sick, we remember how much Jesus loves us. We know that Jesus will always be with us when we are sick. He makes some people well. He helps all people while they are sick. Even when people die, Jesus promises to take them to heaven.

Now we will pray for _____ . His sickness has given us a chance to think about the ways Jesus loves us.

Birth of a Baby

(Use this devotion after a baby has been born to the family of one of the students or a member of the staff.)

The Word
Your praise reaches up to the heavens; it is sung by children and babies. Psalm 8:1b, 2a

The World
Gifts for the baby—clothing, toys, etc. A picture of the baby, if practical.

Today I have happy news to share with you. (Tell about the birth of the baby. Let the member of the baby's family tell the name, date of birth, and other details.)

I have some gifts for the new baby. See, this gift is for _____ to wear. When the baby wears this gift, I'll be sharing in her (his) life. I'll be helping her look pretty and feel comfortable. This is a toy for _____ . When she plays with the toy, I'll be helping her have fun. I'll be helping her learn to enjoy life.

We give gifts to others to share in their lives. That's why I have these gifts for the new baby.

But these two things are not the only gifts we have to talk about today. The baby is also a gift. (Show the picture.) The baby is a gift from God to the _____ family. God gave the gift to this family because He wants to share His love with the

48

family. When God gave _____ to this family, He gave each person in the family someone to love. And He gave each person in the family another person to love them.

Do you know you were also a gift from God to your family? When you were born, your family was happy just as the _____ family is happy today. Your family's friends were happy for your family. The people at church were glad that God gave you to your family and your family to you.

God gave you to one family. Today we're glad that God gave _____ to the _____ family. But God gave one Baby to every family. Jesus also came to earth as a baby. He was born into a family with a mother and a father. But God gave Jesus to all families. He is the Savior, who is God's special gift to everyone.

Because Jesus is our Savior, we can enjoy the gift of new babies into our families. We're happy about the birth of _____ today. To show our happiness we give her gifts.

The baby cannot say "thank you" for these gifts. But she can enjoy them. That will be her way of saying thanks. The Bible reading for today says that a baby can also sing praises to God. The new baby cannot sing songs like we do in chapel. But her happiness is a song of praise to God. Even when she cries, she is singing praise to God, because God has given her a mother and a father, brothers and/or sisters, to help her.

Baptism

(Use this devotion during the week prior to a baptismal service. Invite the schoolchildren to be present at the baptism as a group. They might also sing at the baptismal service.

The Word
Peter said to them, "Each one of you must turn away from his sins and be baptized in the name of Jesus Christ, so that your sins will be forgiven; and you will receive God's gift, the Holy Spirit. For God's promise was made to you and your children, and to all who are far away—all whom the Lord our God calls to Himself." Acts 2:38-39

The World
Baptismal certificate, napkin, water.

I'm getting ready for church next Sunday. Something very special will happen at the _____ o'clock service. I invite all of you to be at the big event. (Tell who is to be baptized and identify relationships with students.)

We have to get ready for the baptism. Do you know what this is (certificate)? You probably have something just like this at home. It is a certificate to remind you that you are baptized. I have a certificate here for each person to be baptized on Sunday. See, their names are here, the date, who their sponsors are, and where they were baptized. If you would like to know about your baptism, ask your parents to show you your certificate.

To get ready for the baptism next Sunday I also need this (water and napkins). I'll put the water in the baptismal font. To baptize means to wash. So we use water to wash. When we wash, we need to dry; so I have the napkins to dry each person who will be baptized.

I can get these things ready for the baptism next Sunday, but I cannot prepare for the most important part of baptism. Someone else had to do that. What else do I need for a baptism? (Help the children answer that you need someone to be baptized.)

Jesus helps us get ready for this baptism. He died on the cross to pay for our sins. If He hadn't done that, baptism wouldn't do any good and no one would come to be baptized. When we are baptized, we received the forgiveness of sins. Jesus gives us faith in Himself. When we are baptized, we receive God's gift, the Holy Spirit, who gives us that faith. Jesus promises us the gift of the Holy Spirit and the forgiveness of sins through our baptism. (Read the first verse of the text.)

Jesus also invites us to be baptized. He says the promise of baptism is for children and for all whom the Lord God calls to Himself. God has called you to be with Him. That's why you have been baptized. God calls these people whose names are on the certificates to be with Him. That's why they will be baptized. God calls all other people to receive His gift of baptism too. (Read the second verse of the text.)

We are happy to be a part of the baptism next Sunday because we are happy for those who will be baptized. But we're also happy because these baptisms will remind us that we also are baptized. God has called us to be with Him too.

At the Time of Death

(This devotion may be used when one of the students has a death in the family or a funeral is held at the church. It should be adapted to the individual situation.)

The Word

For surely you know that when we are baptized into union with Christ Jesus, we were baptized into union with His death. Romans 6:3

The World

A stuffed animal, an adult.

Do you like to go places alone? I don't. I like to go places with other people. What would school be like if you were the only student—just you and the teacher? It's more fun to have lots of boys and girls in school together.

What about when you go to bed? Do you like to take a stuffed animal like this one to bed with you? Or do you have a favorite blanket or pillow to help you go to sleep? Many children want a toy or favorite blanket with them when they go to bed.

Or suppose you're going to a movie. The sign says, "Children free when with an adult." If you want to see the movie, you have to be with your mother, father, or another adult. Let's borrow this adult (a staff person). By yourself, you couldn't get in. But if you were with this adult, you could see the movie. You need someone with you.

You will also need someone with you when you die. We don't have to be afraid to talk about dying, because someone will be with us. It would be nice to have the stuffed animal with you, but someone else will also be with you. If you were dying, your parents, doctors, and others who care for you would be with you, but even Someone else has promised to be with you.

Listen to what the Bible says, "For surely you know that when we were baptized into union with Christ Jesus, we were baptized into union with His death."

Jesus wants to be with you when you die. That's one reason He asked for you to be baptized in His name. Jesus has already died. He went to death alone. He died in our place, so we don't have to die alone. By our baptism we are in union with Jesus. He is with us—even when we die. (Apply the death of Jesus to the person who died recently. The person was not alone. Jesus was with the person at death.)

I pray that you will live for many years. But all of us will die sometime. We tell you about Jesus so you can live with Him now. Even though we can't see Him, He is with us. He promised to be with us at all times. We hear His Word when we read the Bible. We talk to Him when we pray.

He's with us now, and He'll be with us when we die. Remember that you could get into the movie for free when you were with an adult. God says you can get into heaven for free when you are with Jesus. And He has promised to be with you.

Evangelism

The Word

Jesus said to them, "Come with Me, and I will teach you to catch men." At once they left their nets and went with Him. Matthew 4:19-20

The World

"IT" printed on a piece of paper, and a pad of paper with a cross drawn on each page (if practical, the pad should have a sheet for each student).

Do you know how to play tag? I'll show you. I am "it." So you can see that I am "it," I'll hold this piece of paper in front of me. See this word. The word is "It." So I am "it."

When we play tag and I am "it," I must touch someone else. When I touch someone, that person is "it." See, I will touch Sean. Now he is "it." (Give him the piece of paper.) I am not "it" anymore. Sean is "it."

Because Sean is "it," he must catch someone else. When he touches another person, that one becomes "it." (Help the first child pass the paper on to another child.) Now Sean is not "it." Cindy is "it."

Jesus once did something that's like a game of tag. He helped some fishermen catch lots of fish. Then He told them to stop fishing and to follow Him. He said He would teach them to catch people. The men knew how to catch fish. But they did not know how to catch people. Jesus said He would teach them how to catch people. He also teaches us to play His special game of tag.

Jesus starts the game. He is "it." (Show the pad with a cross drawn on each page.) Jesus is "it" because He is our Savior. He loves us. He died to pay for our sins. He rose from the dead to give us a new life that will last forever. Jesus gives us all these gifts when He reaches out and touches us with His love. He gives us His forgiveness. He promises to take us to heaven with Him.

Jesus touched those fishermen on the day He helped them catch fish. When He tagged them, they became "it." (Tear off one page of the pad. Keep the single page and give the pad to a child.) Now I've given you the cross. The cross tells you that Jesus is your Savior. Because you have the cross, you are "it." You are the one who is supposed to catch other people. You are like the fishermen. You are to catch people.

(Help the child give the pad to another—but tear off one sheet for the first child to keep.) Now Pete is "it." He has the cross. But look—Jill is still "it" too. She still has a cross. And I am still "it" too, because I still have a cross.

We catch other people for Jesus when we tell them that Jesus loves them. Telling people about Jesus is like a game of tag because we are catching people for Jesus.

But telling others about Jesus is also different from tag. When you play tag, you're no longer "it" after you catch someone else. But when you catch people for Jesus by giving them your faith, you still have faith. You can give your faith to others by telling them about Jesus, but you still have faith in Him.

Jesus has sent people to tell us about Jesus. Today I am fishing for people when I tell you about the Savior. You also can tell others. Jesus wants us all to work with Him.

Worship

The Word
Jesus [said], "How happy are those who hear the Word of God and obey it!" Luke 11:28

The World
A piece of paper, for each person, with the message: Jesus Loves Me.

We come to chapel each week to worship Jesus. We worship Jesus when we listen to Him speak to us and when we speak to Him.

Do you know how you can talk to Jesus? (Let the students talk about praying and singing. Include not only prayers of request but also praise and thanksgiving.)

How does Jesus talk to you when you worship? (Help them see that He talks through others—others who tell them the message God gives in the Bible.)

Listen to what the Bible tells you. Jesus said, "How happy are those who hear the Word of God and obey it!" We want to help you be happy as you worship. I like to see you look happy when you come to chapel. Your smiles are part of your worship. You're happy to be with Jesus. You're happy to be with friends who also love Jesus.

Let's see if what Jesus says will work for us as we worship today. He says we will be happy if we hear His Word. His Word tells us that He loves us. Because He loves us He came to live with us. Because He loves us He died for our sins. Because He loves us He stays with us today.

Now you have heard God's Word. Did it make you happy? Are you happy to know that Jesus loves you and is your Savior? Jesus is right. When we hear His Word we are happy.

However, Jesus also told us to obey His Word. We are to hear His Word and obey it. How do you obey a message that says Jesus loves you? You obey it when you remember His love. When you love Him, you obey His Word. When you love other people, you obey His Word. To obey His Word you keep the Word with you and you remember His love all the time.

You have heard the Word that tells you Jesus loves you. Now let me give you the Word so you may obey it by keeping it with you. (Give each child the words printed on paper.) Most of you can't read yet; so let me tell you what the message is. (Go over each word. Help them see and understand the message.)

How are you going to keep that Word? You've heard that Jesus loves you. Where will you keep the Word? (Let them talk about places they might keep the paper. In each case give a way it could be lost.)

There is one place you could keep it and never lose it. In your heart. Keep the message that Jesus loves you in your heart and you'll never lose it.

Each time we worship, Jesus will talk to you and you will talk to Him. He will love you. You will love Him. And you'll be happy.

One in Christ

The Word
So there is no difference between Jews and Gentiles, between slaves and free men, between men and women; you are all one in union with Christ Jesus. Galatians 3:28

The World
The children.

All of you who have birthdays this month raise your hand.
If you have a brother, raise your hand.
If you have a sister, raise your hand.
Everyone who is wearing something blue raise your hand.
All the boys raise your hand.
If Jesus loves you, raise your hand.
All the girls raise your hand.
If you have a dog at home, raise your hand.
If you have a cat at home, raise your hand.
If you are wearing something red, raise your hand.
If Jesus died for you and came back to life for you, raise your hand.
Do you see how different we are from one another? Some are boys and some

are girls. You have different kinds of clothing, different colors of hair. When I asked you to raise your hand to show something about yourself, some hands would go up and some would not. (Illustrate by showing that in answering the questions a boy and girl were alike if their birthday was the same month, but were different in other ways.)

But did you notice the times when everyone raised their hand? What did I ask when everyone raised their hand?

That's right, when I asked about Jesus, you were all alike. Jesus loves all of you. Jesus died for each of you to take away your sins. Jesus rose from the dead for all of you; so all of you can be with Him in heaven.

It's okay for us to be different from other people. You can like different kinds of food, have a different color of skin, speak a different language. Some of you can sing. Some can play ball. Some can draw pictures. Others can tell stories. Each of you is different in special ways

But on one important subject, we are all alike. The Bible says: "There is no difference between Jews and Gentiles, between slaves and free men, between men and women; you are all one in union with Christ Jesus."

In Jesus there is no difference between you and a little baby, between you and a grandmother. You are one in Jesus Christ because He loves all of you. You may be rich or poor, big or little, healthy or sick, the student who gets good grades or the student who gets poor grades, but you are all one in Jesus Christ.

Now everyone who loves Jesus, put up your hand. We can all be alike because we love Him. We can love Him because He first loved all of us.

A Word About Words

The Christian faith is expressed in words. We read words in the Bible. We speak words to others. We listen to the words of others. This book depends on the writing and reading of words.

Many words used by Christians have special meanings because the action of Jesus Christ has been added to the word. Devotions in this section give special attention to the words: grace, faith, love, hope, confess, and forgive. All these words are used in our everyday lives. But each word has a special meaning when Christ becomes a part of its context.

Often Christians have a difficult time defining basic theological words. They sense rather than know the spiritual definition.

These devotions are to help small children get a grasp of both the feeling and the meaning of basic Christian concepts. The definitions of the words used in these devotions are beginnings—not final answers. The explanations are intended to give the basic understanding of a word for the child to use as he or she continues a lifetime of growth in understanding the deep mysteries of God as He has let us know Him in Jesus Christ.

These devotions are intended to be used throughout the school year. Plan your schedule far enough ahead so those that are written as a series on the same word may be used without interruption. These devotions may be used when one of the words is needed to help the children understand an important concept in a Bible story being used in the classrooms. Or these devotions may be used to fill in the gaps between special events in the church and school year activities.

But these devotions are not just fillers. Use a Covenant Box (directions for making below) with each devotion in this section. The Covenant Box will be a signal to the children that the devotion is going to teach a special word.

Follow the directions in Exodus 25:10-22 (TEV) to make the Covenant Box. You may use a convenient box, but it would be better to make one the exact size and shape as the original. Use cardboard or Masonite in place of acacia wood, paint instead of gold, and broomsticks or cane fishing rods instead of acacia poles. Make angels from paper or use figures of angels from another source. Print COVENANT BOX in large letters on one side.

Print the following words on large posters and place them in the Covenant Box with the object that is to illustrate the word:

GRACE: A gift box that may be opened and closed.

FAITH: A rope and a cross.

LOVE: A picture of the students, a picture of Jesus, and two picture frames that may be fastened together.

HOPE: A cloth sack with a cross inside.

CONFESS: A pitcher that does not reveal its contents.

FORGIVE: A roll of paper towels.

Other items may be needed for some devotions (and are listed under "The World"), but these words and items should be kept in the Covenant Box. The staff may want to prepare other devotions to help children understand other important theological words. Add the word and the object that symbolizes it to the Covenant Box.

Do not use the Covenant Box to hold objects used for devotions that do not fit into this series. Keep the Covenant Box as a symbol to the children. The presence of the Covenant Box will tell them they are going to learn a new word or review a word they have learned.

Classes in the school may take turns being custodians of the Covenant Box. Children from the class in charge may carry the Box to the front of the church on the days it is to be used. They should carry it in after the other children are seated and remove it before the worshipers leave the church.

Teachers may also use the Covenant Box during the Bible story time in the classroom. After a word has been introduced in a chapel service, the word and the object remain in the Box. The Covenant Box may be carried from classroom to classroom for the teachers' use.

The Covenant Box

Make the Covenant Box according to the directions given in Exodus 25:10-22.

The angels may be made of cardboard. Enlarge the diagrams of the body and wings so the completed angels' wings will touch. Use Styrofoam balls for the angels' heads.

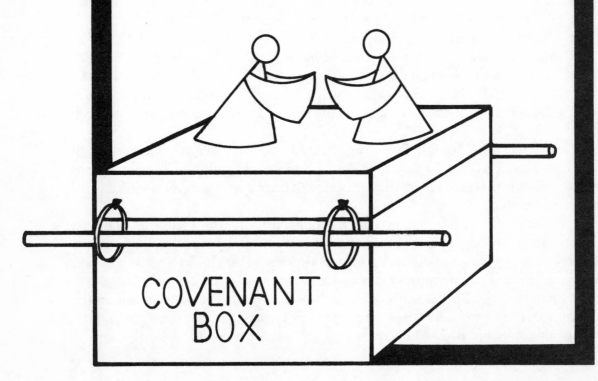

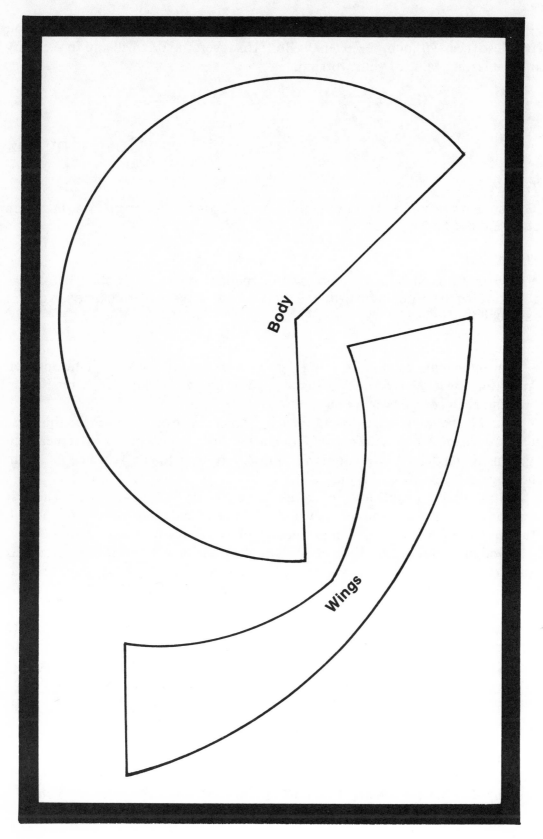

Body

Wings

Note to worship leaders: The devotions in this section are presented so you could use them without the Covenant Box. However, the Box will add to the unity and the lasting value of your worship.

Covenant Box

The Word
[God said to Moses], "Put the two stone tablets inside the Box and put the lid on top of it." Exodus 25:21

The World
A Covenant Box made according to the directions given in Exodus 25:10-22, as amended in the introduction to this section. A cookie, piece of fruit, or token gift for each child.

I want to make a deal with you. I'll give you a cookie if you can lift me up when I'm sitting down. Would you take that deal? You know you can't lift me up. So you wouldn't get a cookie even if you tried.

But I do have enough cookies for each of you to have one. They are in this Box. It is a Covenant Box. See the name written here. Covenant is a big word. It means an agreement or a deal. A covenant is a promise. I promise to give you a cookie from the Covenant Box if you lift me.

God told His people how to make a Covenant Box a long time ago. The first one was made with gold and special wood. This one is made with cardboard and foil. But this Covenant Box can help us understand the deal God makes with us.

God offered this deal: If we obey all of His law, He will be our God. That was His promise. He told Moses to write the laws down on two tablets of stone and put them in the Covenant Box. The Box reminded the people of God's deal. God will be your God if you do everything He says.

But you can't lift me. And you can't obey all of God's laws. You do some things that are wrong. But God still wants to be your God. So He sent Jesus to be your Savior. Jesus came to obey all of God's laws for us. He kept God's first deal. So God gave us a new deal in Jesus. God is our Father because Jesus died for us and took away our sins. Our Covenant Box does not have the laws of God in it. Instead this Box reminds us of God's new deal.

Remember those cookies. The first deal was that I would give one to you if you lifted me up when I was sitting. You couldn't do it. So I'll do it for you. (Sit down and stand up.) Now I give you a cookie because I want you to have one. You couldn't do what I asked you to do, but I did it for you. Come and get a cookie. (Allow each child to take a cookie from the Box.)

60

Today you took a cookie from the Covenant Box. Next week I'll have something else for you in the Box. It will not be a cookie or anything to eat. It will be something more important. We will use the Covenant Box to remind us of the many gifts God has given to us by the new promise He gave us. Because God sent Jesus to obey the Law in our place, we have many gifts. This Box will remind us of those gifts.

We will always be talking about God's new covenant. Remember that the covenant, see the word here, is God's promise to you. He promises to give you many gifts. And I promise to tell you about them.

Grace

The Word

It is by God's grace that you have been saved. Ephesians 2:5b

The World

A large (at least as big as a shoe box) box wrapped as a gift (not connected with any season or event) so the top can be removed without destroying the wrapping, a child's book, the words BOOK and GRACE each printed on a large sheet of paper.

Do you know what this word (BOOK) is? You have not been taught how to read yet, so I don't expect you to be able to read the word. But if I hold this (the book) with the word, can you guess what it is? That's right. This word is book. B - O - O - K is book.

Now look at this word (GRACE). Do you know what it is? Let's say the letters: G - R - A - C - E. If I show you the word and this (the gift) together, you may be able to guess what the word is.

No, the word is not box. It is not present. The word is not gift, though it means a gift. This word is GRACE. G - R - A - C - E is grace. Remember this gift when you see the word "grace." Grace is a gift from God. Grace can also be a girl's name. Some prayers are called grace. But the first meaning of grace is gift—a present from God to you.

A gift reminds us of grace because gifts are given to show love. People who love you give you gifts. They give you the gift because they want to—not because they have to. You do not earn a gift. You do not pay for a gift. You say "thank you" for a gift and use it.

God's grace is a gift to you. God loves you. He gave you Jesus to forgive your sins. Because God loves you, He sent Jesus to be with you and to stay with you. Jesus brings God's grace to you. You do not earn grace. You do not pay for grace. You just say "thank you" for grace and use it.

This box is empty now. (Show inside of box.) I'll put things in the box for other chapel services. But for now I want to help you remember the word GRACE. When you saw the book, you knew the word BOOK. When you see a gift, you can remember GRACE. Grace is God's gift to you.

God gives you many gifts. All of them are signs of His grace. First of all, He gave you yourself; because He created you. He gives you a family, food, a place to live, our school. He gives you love and forgiveness through Jesus. And because Jesus is your Savior, He gives you a life that will last forever.

All of these and other gifts come from God's grace. Can you imagine all of God's gifts in this box? The box could not hold all the things God gives you. But the box can remind you that God loves you and gives you gifts.

Grace—Not Pay

The Word
It [your place in heaven] is not the result of your own efforts, but God's gift, so that no one can boast about it. Ephesians 2:9

The World
The gift box previously used. The word GRACE on paper. A quarter, a dollar bill and a five-dollar bill.

Do you remember this word (GRACE)? We talked about the word once before. To help you remember the word, I showed you this (the gift). This word is grace. Grace is a gift that you have not earned. Everything that God gives you is a gift of grace. He loves you and blesses you. You have not worked for His love and blessings. They are gifts of grace.

Let's talk about the differences between a gift and wages. Wages are something you work for. Your father and mother may work for a salary. Or they may have their own business to make money. When they work, they earn the money they receive. That money is not a gift. They've earned it.

You may also work to earn money. Maybe you've done a special job to help your mother and father. They may have given you money to pay you for your work. If you took out the garbage every day, your mother might give you this (the quarter). It's a quarter and is worth 25 cents. That would be your wages.

If you did even more work, you might get this (dollar bill). This is a dollar bill. It's worth 100 cents. If you had an even bigger job and you worked hard for a long time, you might get this (five-dollar bill). It's a five-dollar bill. It's worth 500 pennies.

When you work for wages, you get more money if you work harder. The person who worked for five dollars did more than the one who received one dollar. The

63

person who received one dollar worked more than the one who received the quarter.

When you receive a gift like this (show the box), it does not show how hard you have worked. Instead the gift shows how hard the one who gives it has worked. When you receive a good gift, you can't brag that you worked hard to earn it. Someone gave it to you. The person who gave you the gift loved you. When you receive a gift, it does not show that you worked hard. Instead the gift shows that someone loves you.

Jesus worked hard to give you God's gift of grace. He came to earth and lived with us. He was hurt and He died. He came back to life again. He earned something worth more than this money and all other money put together. He earned the way to heaven for all people. When He died for us, He paid for our sins. Now He gives us what He has earned. He gives us forgiveness of sins. He gives us a place in heaven. His gifts are grace to us. We didn't work for them. He worked for them and gave them to us.

When someone gives you wages to pay you for work, you see the money and know you've earned it. But when you receive gifts from God, you see His grace and know that He loves you. God is not paying you for your work. He is loving you by giving you a gift.

Grace—Not a Prize

The Word
It [your place in heaven] is not the result of your own efforts, but God's gift, so that no one can boast about it. Ephesians 2:9

The World
The gift box previously used. The word GRACE on paper. A trophy, from bowling, little league, etc. Dollar bill.

See this word (GRACE)? Do you remember what it is? The word is grace. Please say the word with me: Grace. You can say the word. Do you remember what it means? Grace is an important word. The word grace tells you how God saves you. It tells you how God wants to help you all the time.

To help you remember what it means, I have three things here for you to look at. See, I have a dollar bill, a gift, and a prize. Sue, will you come up and pick up one of these three things to help us remember what grace means? One of these three things helps us remember what grace is. Put that thing here by the word. The rest of you watch Sue. See if you would pick the same thing she picks.

(If the child picks the gift first, follow the order of explanation as given below. If not, reverse and explain the wrong examples first.)

64

That's right. Grace is a gift. Grace is a gift from God. God gave Jesus to us to be our Savior. Jesus gives us love and forgiveness. These things are gifts from God. We do not earn presents. People who love us give us presents. Grace is a present from God, who loves us.

Let's put the word "grace" and the gift together. They belong together. The dollar bill does not belong with the word "grace." The dollar does not help us understand grace. The dollar is a payment. If you work, you earn the dollar. That is not grace. You buy something with a dollar. That is not grace. Grace is a gift.

Now look at this (the prize). This is a prize. The person who was on the team that got the highest score won this prize. We like to win prizes. A prize shows that we can do something well. A prize shows we are winners.

Could we say that the prize is like grace? Does God save you because you're on the winning team? Does God take you to heaven because you won over someone else?

No. Grace is not a prize. Grace is not a reward given only to those who did the best. It is not just for those who were on the right team. You have to work hard to win a prize. You have to practice. You have to follow the rules.

But Christ earned the prize for you. He worked hard. He followed the rules. He won the game. He died and won a victory over death so He could live again. We win only because Christ has won for us and shares His victory with us. We have the prize because Christ won it and gave it to us as a gift. (Put the prize in the gift box.) Now we can have the prize of heaven because it's a gift. It's God's gift to you through Jesus.

Faith

The Word
You have been saved through faith. Ephesians 2:8

The World
A ball, a rope, the word "ball" printed on a piece of typing paper, the word "faith" on another piece of typing paper.

I know you're not able to read yet, but look at this word anyway. (Show the word "ball.") When you see the word by itself, you don't know what it is. But when I show you this (the ball), you can figure out what the word is. This is a ball—a real ball. This is the word "ball." The word "ball" makes us think of a real ball. You already know what a ball is. When you see the ball with the word, you also know the word "ball."

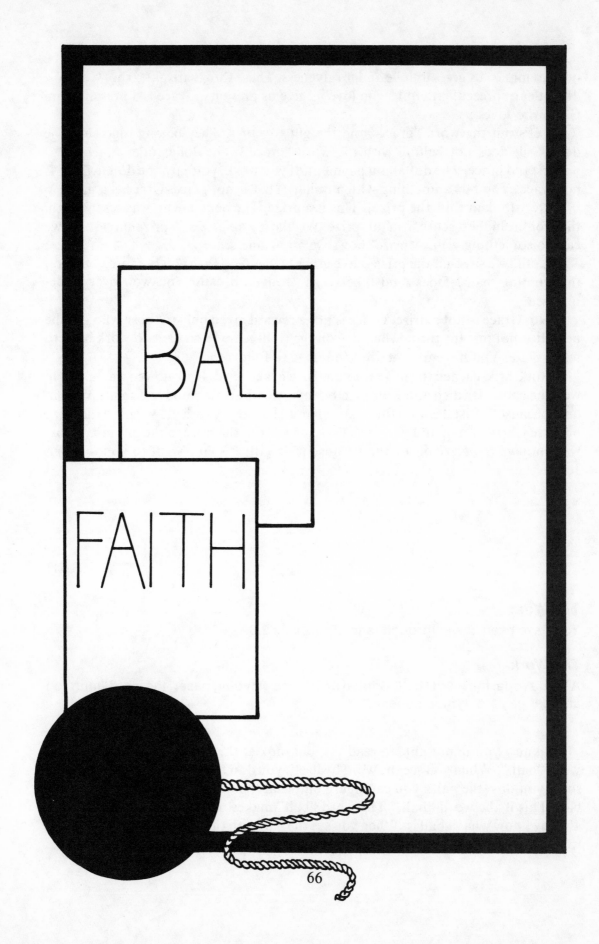

66

Now I want to show you another word. See this one? (Show the word "faith.")
Do you know this word? Let me show you something else. (Hold up the rope.) No,
this word is not "rope." You are right, this is a rope. But we will use the rope to help
you remember this special word.

The word is "faith." Faith is like a rope. Let me show you how faith is like a
rope. Suppose you fell into the water and could not swim. You would drown. But if I
threw this to you (throw the rope to a child and ask the child to hold one end while
you hold the other), what would happen? You'd grab the rope. Would you drown if
you held on to the rope? No, the rope would save you. See, the rope could save any
one of you. (Throw the end of the rope to as many of the children as possible. Let
them pull on the rope. Show how it will lift them. Let others see how strong and
tense the rope is when it is pulled.)

Faith is like the rope, because faith saves you. The Bible says: "You have been
saved through faith." Faith means you hold on to Jesus like you held on to the rope.
If you were in the water and I threw you the rope, you would trust me to pull you out
of the water. If you're afraid, or lonely, or you know you've done something wrong,
God sends Jesus to help you. When you believe Him, you have faith in Him. That
faith is like a rope. It will save you.

You can't see faith—but you can see this rope. So I want you to remember the
rope as a reminder of faith. See—this is the word "faith." Faith is real even though
you can't see it.

I'm going to put the rope on the altar. And I will put the word "faith" on the
rope so you can remember this is a special rope. It reminds you that Jesus saves you.

Faith in Jesus

The Word
Believe in the Lord Jesus, and you will be saved. Acts 16:31

The World
A rope, the word "faith" printed on a piece of typing paper, a cross.

Do you remember what this word is? (Show paper. If some children remember
the word, talk about its meaning. If not, continue.) Maybe this will help you
remember. (Show the rope.) You are right, this is a rope. But this word is not "rope."
The rope reminds us of the word on the paper. If you were in the water and I threw
you the rope, the rope would save you. If you're afraid, lonely, or know you've done
something wrong, God helps you by giving you Jesus. When you grab hold of Jesus,
you have faith in Him. This word is "faith."

Faith means to believe in something, to trust something. If you were in the water and could not swim, you would drown. But if I threw you the rope, you would grab on to the rope. You would trust me to pull the rope and lift you out of the water. That's why the rope reminds us of faith. If you held on to the rope, you would be saved. The Bible tells us that we are saved by faith.

Now let's pretend you're in the water. I throw you the rope. (Throw one end of the rope to a child.) You grab the rope. Are you saved now? (Let the children talk about the answer. Help them think about the sureness of the child who is holding on to the rope. How does he know he is safe?) What would happen if I let loose of this end of the rope? (Have the rope pulled taut and let loose of it suddenly.) Would you be saved then? What would happen?

If you hold on to one end of the rope, you can be saved—as long as someone has a hold on the other end of the rope. The rope will not save you by itself. The rope only gives you a way to be pulled by whoever has the other end.

Your faith also has to hold on to something. Faith is like a rope that is tied to Jesus. (Tie one end of the rope to the cross.) You remember that Jesus died for you and rose again from the dead. This cross is a reminder of His death and of His coming back to live with us again. When you have faith in Jesus, you know that He died for you; so your sins are forgiven. When you know you've done something wrong, you remember that Jesus has paid for your sin. By holding on to Him you are saved.

Jesus is still alive. He is with you to help you when you are lonely or afraid. By faith you can hold on to Him, and He helps you.

Think of faith as a rope. You are holding on to one end. Jesus is at the other end. You can trust Jesus because He will not drop His end of the rope.

Grace and Faith

The Word
For it is by God's grace that you have been saved through faith. Ephesians 2:8

The World
The words GRACE and FAITH. The gift, rope, and cross previously used, with the rope inside the gift box.

Do you remember this word (GRACE)? What is it? What does it mean? (Show the gift to help the children remember grace. Help them define grace as a gift from God.)

Now what is this word (FAITH)? What does it mean? (Help the children define the word. Do not show the rope but ask them if they remember what item was used to illustrate faith.) Why does the rope make you think of faith?

Now let's put the words "grace" and "faith" together. The Bible says you are saved by God's grace. You belong to God because He gave Himself to you.

The Bible also says you are saved by faith. You are saved because you trust in Jesus. You know He loves you and takes away your sin.

How are you saved: by grace or faith? Both, of course. But how do grace and faith work together? I'd like to read something from the Bible that talks about both grace and faith. (Read the text. Repeat it in small sections. Have the children repeat it with you in small sections. Help them say the entire sentence.)

Remember grace is God's gift to you. (Place the gift by the cross on the altar.) God's gift of grace comes to you from Jesus because Jesus died for you. He earned the gift that is your grace. (Take the gift from the cross and give it to a child.) The Savior gives each of you the gift of grace.

Because you have grace, you also have many other gifts. Look at this one. (Open the box and take out the rope.) The first gift of grace is faith. When you receive God's gift of grace, you know about Jesus. So you can believe in Him. That's faith. God gives you grace so you can have faith in Him. (Take one end of the rope back to the cross.)

Now the rope reaches back to the place we started. God gave you grace from Jesus Christ. Now you believe in Jesus and you have a way to go back to Him.

Grace and faith are partners. First God gives you His grace. Then you have faith in Him.

Jesus Loves Us

The Word
See how much the Father has loved us! His love is so great that we are called God's children—and so, in fact, are we. 1 John 3:1a

The World
The word LOVE on a poster. Picture of the speaker's family. A picture of the schoolchildren (use group class picture or a Polaroid snapshot of the class) in a frame that can later be connected to another framed picture.

Do you know this word? Spell it with me: L, O, V, E. The word is love. Whom do you love? Who loves you?

We show our love for each other in many ways. Can you tell me some ways you love people and people love you? (Help the children talk about the way they love parents by hugging, kissing, sitting on laps. Talk about helping, listening, giving gifts. Talk about being together.)

I have another way to show my love for my family. See—this is a picture of (show picture of your family and explain how you keep the picture in your office, purse, or billfold). Why do I keep this picture of my family? That's right. Because I love them. I like to think about them often.

Who has a picture of you? Do your mother and father have your picture? your grandparents? Who else has your picture?

Look at this picture. It's a picture of you and all the other kids in our school. We can pretend this is God's picture of us. God doesn't need to keep a picture of us because He can always see us and be with us. And when He sees us, that's even better than a picture. We can think of His being with us all the time as Him having a picture of us. God loves us, and He wants to see us and think of us—just as our parents do. God likes to look at us. He likes to remember us all the time.

Listen to what the Bible says: "See how much the Father has loved us! His love is so great that we are called God's children—and so, in fact, we are." God is our Father. We are His children. Even though we have sinned, He is our Father because He sent Jesus to pay for our sins. We belong to God because Jesus is our Savior.

Think of God having this picture of you. God always sees you. He does not forget you. He stays with you all the time. He forgives you when you sin. He helps you when you're in trouble. He enjoys your good times with you. He is part of your life.

Remember the word that goes with the picture. The word is LOVE. The Bible says that God loves you so much that He has made you His children. He keeps a picture of you with Him always.

We Love Jesus

The Word
We love because God first loved us. 1 John 4:19

The World
The word LOVE on a poster. The picture of the children in a frame and a picture of Jesus in another frame that can later be connected to the first. If practical, have a picture of Jesus for each child to take home.

Do you remember what this word is (LOVE)? How do you know when a person loves you? (Talk about the way others show their love to us. Include the idea that people who love you often have a picture of you.) Remember this picture (the children)? We used it as a reminder that God loves you. He sees you and is with you. He enjoys you. That's like having a picture of you to remind Him of His love for you.

Now listen to what the Bible says: "We love because God first loved us."

(Repeat the text in short phrases and have the children say it with you. Then help them say the entire verse several times.)

First God loves us. He has made us. He gave us our bodies, minds, and souls. He loves us even when we do wrong things. Jesus died on the cross to pay for our sins. He loves and helps us in all our needs.

We said that God has a picture of us because He loves us. Now remember that the Bible verse said, "We love because God first loved us." If He loves us and has a picture of us, we can love Him and have a picture of Him.

See this picture (Jesus)? Do you know who this is? It's Jesus. Jesus is God. He is also a person like us. We can't have a picture of God, because God is too great for a picture. But Jesus became a person like us so we can know God. God loved us and sent Jesus to show us that love. When we love Jesus, we also love God.

We often have pictures of Jesus to remind us of His love for us. When we think about the way Jesus loves us, we also love Him. A picture of Jesus reminds us both that He loves us and that we love Him.

Where do you see pictures of Jesus? (Talk about pictures of the Savior in classrooms, homes, lessons, Bibles, etc. If available, give each student a picture of Jesus for his or her bedroom.)

Always let the picture of Jesus remind you of love. First of His love for you, Then of your love for Him.

Love Together

The Word

Dear friends, if this is how God loved us, then we should love one another. We are sure that we live in union with God and that He lives in union with us, because He has given us His Spirit. 1 John 4:11 and 13

The World

The word LOVE on a poster. The two pictures (Jesus and the schoolchildren) in frames that can be fastened together.

How many of you remember this word (LOVE)? Tell me about love. (Let the children share ideas about love.)

We can talk about love. But love is more than what we say. Love is what we do. Seth, would you come up and help me? Show me what love is. (Stand far away from the child. Repeat the instructions by asking him to show love by what he does rather than what he says.)

That's hard to do, isn't it, Seth? You can't show love by yourself. But if I'm with you, you can show love. (Stoop or sit down to be on the same level as the child.

Illustrate ways to show love: talk together, touch, shake hands, hug. Explain that being together is showing love.) You cannot love by yourself. To love you always have to be with another person.

Because God loves us (show picture of children) and we love God (show picture of Jesus), we are together. (Fasten the pictures together.) Our love brings us together. People often have pictures taken together or fastened together. Husbands and wives have their pictures together. Brothers and sisters have their pictures together. This picture of our students shows all of you together. When we put the picture of Jesus and you together, we show what love does for us. We are with Jesus. He is with us.

Listen to what the Bible says: "Dear friends, if this is how God loved us, then we should love one another." Jesus loves me. Jesus loves you. So we can love each other. Jesus loves all people, so His love brings us together with all people.

Sometimes we don't want to love other people. We cannot pretend we love them. Instead remember that Jesus loves you. Then remember that Jesus loves the other person. Because you are with Jesus, you are with everyone that Jesus loves.

The Bible also says, "We are sure that we live in union with God and that He lives in union with us, because He has given us His Spirit." We can be sure we love God, because He loves us. When He loves us He gives us the Holy Spirit, who helps us receive love and helps us give love.

Your picture and Jesus' picture belong together. Love holds you and Jesus together. That love also helps you love others.

Hope

The Word
For it was by hope that we were saved; but if we see what we hope for, then it is not really hope. For who hopes for something he sees? Romans 8:24

The World
The word HOPE on a poster. A cross in a cloth sack, a ball.

Let's learn another new word today. This word is HOPE. Would you spell it with me? H . . . O . . . P . . . E. Tell me ways you use the word "hope." (Help the children finish the sentence, "I hope . . .") Now think about all the things you hope for. They are things you don't have now.

(Show the ball.) Would it be right for me to say, "I hope this is a ball"? No. I don't hope this is a ball. I know it is a ball. I can see it. I can touch it. It is a ball.

Now look at this sack. Something is in the sack. I cannot see it. I cannot feel it—but I can feel what it's like. (Invite several children to feel the cross in the sack.) What's in the sack? How do you know? (Let the children explain that they can know that it's a cross even though they have not seen it.) We don't know what color the cross is. We don't know if it has words printed on it. Our knowing about the cross is like hope. It's something we are sure of, even though we have not seen it.

Our Bible reading for today says we are saved by hope. We hope Jesus will take us to heaven. We hope we will live with Him forever. We have not seen Jesus yet. We have not been to heaven yet. But we hope for the time we will see Him in heaven. The Bible reading also says that if we see what we hope for it is not really hope. Then it asks, "For who hopes for something he sees?"

When we are in heaven, we will be saved. We will no longer hope for salvation. We will have it. I know this is a ball; I do not have to hope it is a ball. In heaven I will know Jesus. I will not have to hope I will know Him.

But now we live by hope. We are not in heaven yet. But our hope is not just a dream. We do not depend on luck. Our hope is in Jesus. We are saved not just because we want to be saved, but because Jesus died for us and rose again from the dead to give us life. He has already done that. We don't have to hope He will do it. He has done it. What He has done gives us hope for what He will do.

Our salvation is like the cross in this sack. Even though we cannot see the cross, we know it's there. We know the size and shape of the cross even though we have not seen it.

We also have hope that Jesus will take us to heaven, because we already know He came to be with us on earth. We know what He has done, so we can have hope in what He will do.

The cross in the sack helps us know what the word "hope" means. Hope in Jesus tells us we can be sure about something we have not yet seen.

Hope with Patience

The Word

For it was by hope that we were saved; but if we see what we hope for, then it is not really hope. For who hopes for something he sees? But if we hope for what we do not see, we wait for it with patience. Romans 8:24-25

The World

The word HOPE on a poster. A cross in a cloth sack, a large closed box.

Remember this word (HOPE)? What does H . . . O . . . P . . . E spell? Hope is an important word for us because the Bible says, "It was by hope that we were saved."

If hope helps us understand how we will go to heaven, we had better know what hope means. First, let's look at this box. Do you know what's in it? You can't see what's in the box. Listen as I shake it. That doesn't help.

What do you hope is in the box? (Let the children talk about food, toys, books, etc.)

Sometimes hope means, "I don't know," or "I'm not sure." When you say you hope something is in this box, you mean you don't know. But that is not the kind of hope that saves us. Our hope is in Jesus Christ. We know Him. Our hope is not like something in a box that we cannot see.

Instead our hope is like this (sack). Can you see what's in the sack? But you can feel what's in the sack. Try it. (Have several children handle the sack.) What's in it? It's a cross. The cross is a reminder that Jesus died for our sins. The cross tells us that Jesus rose from the dead.

Look at both the box and the sack. You can't see what's in either of them. But you can hope. If you hope for something in the box, you are only guessing. But if you hope for the cross in the sack, you are not guessing. Even though you have not seen what's in the sack, you have felt the cross. You can hope for the cross because you know about it.

Our hope in Jesus is like the cross in the sack. We know what Jesus has done. He died for us. He rose from the dead. Even though we have not seen Him, we know what He has done. We also know what He has promised to do. He has promised to be with us today. He has promised to take us to heaven.

So we live in hope. Our Bible reading says, "If we hope for what we do not see, we wait for it with patience." You do not have to worry about what God has for you. You can be patient because you have hope. Your hope is in Jesus.

Confess Faith

The Word
If you confess that Jesus is Lord and believe that God raised Him from death, you will be saved. Romans 10:9

The World
The word CONFESS on a poster, a pitcher (which does not reveal its contents) filled with lemonade, a glass.

Here's another word for you to learn (CONFESS). The word is CONFESS. Say the letters with me: C...O...N...F...E...S...S. The Bible says, "If you confess that Jesus is Lord and believe that God raised Him from death, you will be saved."

Look at this pitcher. It has something in it. Can you tell what it is? But watch.

(Pour out some of the lemonade into the glass and let a student taste it.) What's in the pitcher? How do you know?

You did not know what was in the pitcher until I poured out some of the lemonade. Now you know what's in the pitcher. If I pour out some more, you know it will be lemonade.

You are like this pitcher. I cannot see what's in you. I can't look at you and tell what you are thinking. I don't know what you believe. For me to know what's in you, you have to pour out your faith for me to see. You can tell me what you believe. When you tell me what you believe, you are confessing your faith.

Before I could pour lemonade out of the pitcher, I had to put lemonade into the pitcher. Before you can confess your faith by pouring out what you believe, you have to receive the message of God's love. That's why I tell you about Jesus each time we come to chapel. Remember what I tell you. Jesus loves you. He is with you. He died to pay for your sins. He rose from the dead to give you a new life. He will take you to heaven.

Jesus tells you about Himself so you can believe in Him. That's filling you up with faith. When you confess your faith, you tell others that He loves them. He died for them. He will take them to heaven. When you confess your faith, you pour out to others what Jesus has put in you—just as I put lemonade into the pitcher so I could pour it out.

Do you know how to confess your faith? How can you tell others what Jesus has done for you and them? (Discuss talking to family and friends about Jesus. Remember, we also confess our faith to fellow Christians. Mention songs that confess faith.)

Also in our worship we confess our faith by telling what we believe. I believe Jesus is my Savior. Do you believe that? Let's say it together. (Repeat the line with the students several times.) In our church every Sunday we also confess our faith together as we say we believe in Jesus. You can learn to say that too. You can confess your faith.

Confess Sins

The Word

Then I confessed my sins to You; I did not conceal my wrongdoings. I decided to confess them to You, and You forgave all my sins. Psalm 32:5

The World

The word CONFESS on a poster. A pitcher (that does not reveal its contents) filled with dirty water, a glass.

What does C...O...N...F...E...S...S (show the word) spell? Do you remember what CONFESS means? Remember the pitcher? (Show it.) You cannot see what's in the pitcher. But if I pour what's in it into a glass, you know what it is. To confess is to pour out, to admit, to tell.

We confess our faith when we tell others we believe in Jesus. Because we know Jesus has died for us and lives again, we believe in Him. He gives us faith. We pour our faith out when we confess it.

But faith is only one of the many things in us. We can confess our faith. We also have other things to confess. King David wrote the psalm that is our Bible reading for today. Listen to what he confesses. (Read the text.)

King David had done some bad things. He had sinned. But no one else knew what he had done. His sins were hidden. He did not get caught. He was like this pitcher. You cannot see what's in it. No one could look at King David and see the bad things he had done.

When you look at me, you do not know what I have done wrong. When I look at you, I do not know the bad things you have done. We hide our sins. No one can see them, if we don't get caught.

But King David got tired of hiding his sins. He hurt inside. He felt guilty. So he confessed his sins to God. He admitted to God what he had done wrong. He poured out his sins. (Pour the dirty water into a glass.) See what's in the pitcher. It's dirty water. We did not know the water was dirty until it was poured out. It was hidden. Now we know it's dirty water. We can throw it away and get clean water. If we would hide the dirty water, we would never get clean water.

If we hide our sins, we never get rid of them. If we confess our sins, God forgives us. King David was happy that he confessed his sins. God forgave him. He was free from his sins. He was clean again.

The Bible tells us we should confess our sins. We don't have to hide our sins

77

from God. He knows we do wrong things. Jesus knew that we are sinners. That's why He died for us. He paid for our sins.

When we confess our sins, we give the bad things to Jesus. He forgives us and gives us His goodness.

When you feel sin inside you, think of the pitcher. You can pour the sin out by confessing it to Jesus. He'll make you clean again.

Forgive

The Word
I decided to confess them to You, and You forgave all my sins. Psalm 32:5b

The World
The word FORGIVE on a poster. A pitcher, previously used, filled with dirty water; a roll of paper towels.

Today's word is FORGIVE. Look at the word. Will you say it with me? Forgive. Let's spell it: F . . . O . . . R . . . G . . . I . . V . . . E. Forgive.

Today's Bible verse uses the word "forgive." It also uses another word that we've learned: CONFESS. In the Bible verse King David is talking to God. He says, "I decided to confess them to You, and You forgave all my sins."

David confessed his sins to God. Remember what "confess" means? David poured out his sins to God. (Pour out a little of the dirty water on a table or other suitable surface. If practical, invite the children to stand around the area and watch.) David did not hide his sins; He poured them out to God. When David confessed his sins, God forgave them. (Use a paper towel to wipe up the water.) See what happens. When I wipe up the dirty water, the mess is gone. This is like forgiveness. When we confess our sins, we pour the mess out of ourselves. (Pour out some water.) Then God forgives us by cleaning up the mess we made. (Wipe up the water.)

Notice what God does when He forgives our sins. He takes our mess and puts it on Himself. See these paper towels I used to wipe up the dirty water? They're dirty now. That dirt was in the pitcher. Remember, the pitcher is like you and me. We sin. But when we confess our sins we pour the sins out. But the sins are still there. Then God takes the sins on Himself. He is like the paper towel. He cleans up the mess we made. He forgives our sins.

Jesus comes into our lives to be like the paper towel. We know He is with us. We know He loves us. So we can confess our sins to Him. We pour out our mess on Him. Jesus can take our mess on Himself because He died for our sins. Our sins would destroy us if we kept them to ourselves. But when Jesus takes our sins on Himself (show the dirty towel), He is not destroyed. Even though He had to die because of us, He rose again from the dead. He is alive and with us to forgive our sins. (Show a clean towel.) Jesus is always holy because He is God. But He came to be with us and to wipe up our mess. He forgives our sins.